Of Hartford in Many Lights

Of Hartford in Many Lights

Celebrating Hartford's Buildings

∽

Dennis Barone and Deborah Ducoff-Barone
Editors

GRAYSON BOOKS
West Hartford, Connecticut
graysonbooks.com

Of Hartford in Many Lights: Celebrating Hartford's Buildings
Copyright © 2024 Dennis Barone and Deborah Ducoff-Barone
Published by Grayson Books
West Hartford, Connecticut
ISBN: 979-8-9888186-8-7
Library of Congress Control Number: 2024936659

Cover Image:
James Goodwin McManus
American, 1882-1958
The Traveler's Tower, Hartford, 1919
Oil on canvas, 38 ¼ x 28 ¼ in. (97.2 x 71.8 cm)
Wadsworth Atheneum Museum of Art, Hartford, CT
The Ella Gallup Sumner and Mary Catlin Sumner Collection Fund, 1954.60
Photographed by Allen Phillips/Wadsworth Atheneum

Book and Cover Design by Cindy Stewart

Dedicated to David K. Leff
Environmentalist, Historian, Poet

Contents

The Structures

"Let us build the building of light."
—Wallace Stevens, "Architecture"

Preface

I was running the Hartford Marathon's half-marathon, many moons ago, when my knees still worked. As happens in road races, you run with people who are keeping the same pace as you. There was a fellow from out-of-state, Pennsylvania, if I recall, in my little group. He turned to me at one point and said, "You know, this is a beautiful city."

Indeed!

If we're in a place long enough, we can take it for granted, fail to see what is right in front of our noses. It can take a fresh set of eyes to remind us of the handsome and interesting structures that make the city attractive. But instead of one sweaty guy in shorts, how about hearing from 44 poets?

Imagination is our better angel. Asking poets to write about Hartford's major structures, as Dennis Barone and Deborah Ducoff-Barone have done, is a wonderfully original idea.

The poet and the architect create art. Both start with an idea or vision; draw from earlier sources, if only to break from them; build in stages; and pray that it works. The poems here evoke the work of many of the great architects who worked in Hartford, from Charles Bulfinch (Old State House) to George Keller (Soldiers and Sailors Memorial Arch and many others) the modernist Richard Meier (Hartford International University for Religion and Peace, formerly the Hartford Seminary).

As architects experiment with form, so do poets. For example, the marvelous Bessy Reyna creates a four-part dialogue around an 1837 case argued in the Old State House in which the Supreme Court of Errors, as it was then called, granted a young black woman her freedom.

She poses the intriguing question: "What if we, the Europeans, were the slaves, / and the Africans our masters?"

In a similar vein, Julia M. Paul's poem about the State Supreme Court building intersperses observations about the building with references to some of the great cases and issues that have been debated and decided there.

This raises a question. That building is solid, classical, majestic. Isn't it meant to reflect the importance society gives to the rule of law and the state's highest court? Shouldn't all public buildings aspire to such a standard? Looked at from another angle, did test scores go down when they started building dull, utilitarian school buildings? I wonder.

If you know the Hartford buildings, the poems will evoke memories. The earliest of mine involves the G. Fox Building, department store turned community college. I grew up in New London, but each December we'd make the pilgrimage to G. Fox, as people did from around the state, and the ladies got dressed up to do it. For a kid, the electric trains, the escalators, the vanilla milkshakes in the Connecticut Room— it was so great—except for waiting for my mother while she shopped.

At the age of seven, I believed that the Santa Claus at G. Fox was the real Santa, and that the others were, you might say, independent Clauses. What brought this to mind was Kenneth DiMaggio's "Ode to the G. Fox Department Store in Hartford."

If there is a poetic muse that imbues this book, it is that of Wallace Stevens, the insurance executive who was Hartford's greatest 20th century, perhaps any century, poet. The title "Of Hartford in Many Lights" is a play on the Stevens poem "Of Hartford in a Purple Light." The book has a poem called "Of Stevens and The Hartford in Morning Light" by Richard Deming, which describes Stevens's practice of walking to work from his home on Westerly Terrace to The Hartford, crafting poems in his head and then having his secretary type them up. Apparently, they kept this on the q.t. When Stevens was awarded the Pulitzer Prize for poetry in 1955, one young colleague is said to have remarked, "You mean Wally writes poetry?"

There was an effort some years ago to turn the Stevens home into a house museum. I'm so glad it didn't happen; the house isn't particularly distinctive, and house museums are notoriously difficult to sustain. Instead, a group of poets and others, called The Friends and Enemies of Wallace Stevens, did one better. They created the Wallace Stevens Walk. Starting at 118 Westerly Terrace and going to The Hartford on Asylum Avenue, or vice-versa, are 13 granite blocks, each etched with a stanza from Stevens's well-known poem "Thirteen Ways of Looking at a Blackbird." A wonderful idea, one worthy of its honoree, and much easier to maintain than an old house.

In addition to the poems, Deborah and Dennis have added short essays about each of the structures the poets described. The result is a fascinating look at what is, lest we forget, flaws and all, an historic and interesting city. And in case you thought Hartford poetry died when Wally went to heaven, it didn't.

—Tom Condon

Introduction

Of Hartford in Many Lights includes forty-four poems by contemporary Connecticut poets inspired by particular buildings in the capital city. This commemorative collection celebrates and anticipates the 400th anniversary of Hartford, though, granted—a little bit early. We couldn't quite wait for the 400th and so here we are at the 390th anniversary (roughly) offering a literary ride down Albany Avenue and on to Main Street. We then head in one direction or another—Maple or Wethersfield Ave. It's been 390 years since English settlers led by Thomas Hooker and Samuel Stone settled the area. If such celebration feels a bit premature, how about this: 240 years since the incorporation of Hartford as a city.

Our anthology provides both a panoramic view and a snapshot. The poems take the reader from outskirts to river, from colonial outpost to the 1990s debacle of Colonial Reality. There are poems about structures for government or education; entertainment or healthcare; houses of celebrities and ones of worship. Some poems are almost a straightforward description of a building; others address a site more obliquely—a string of associations, an event that occurred in its past, or a tree in the yard.

Some poets chose to write about the place they work: Capital Community College in the adaptive re-use G. Fox Building or the Life Sciences Center at Trinity College. The choices were not free, random, and unguided. We made a list of 104 significant buildings and poets made choices on a first come first served basis from this list; we believe each poet ended up with his or her first-choice structure. This method of selection resulted in some significant omissions: for example, neither the State Armory nor an Edward T. Hapgood designed house are included herein. One poet based her decision on a love of baseball; another wrote in memory of a grandmother whose "tenement was a center of sorts." Another poet said her chosen building "has chosen me." Some poets who grew up in Hartford spoke to us about the power of their church—and this comment tilted more toward criticism than compliment, than praise. Speaking of churches, Wallace Stevens wrote the late poem "St. Armorer's Church from the Outside" with Hartford's Church of the Good Shepherd in mind. Chase Twichell wrote her poem for this volume on Asylum Hill

Congregational Church where her great-grandfather, Reverend Joseph Twichell, was pastor for close to fifty years.

Buildings break down or get built up: they change. Even a historic house museum changes over time, evolves and grows; alters its purpose. Ciaran Berry told us that Trinity College plans to redevelop the Jacobs Life Sciences Center "sometime over the next few years, so it won't be that odd looking Brutalist thing in the middle of campus anymore." What will happen to Union Station when the failing interstate highway 84 viaduct undergoes reconstruction?

After the poems there are very brief prose descriptions or commentaries written by the volume editors about the buildings. The poem remains here primary and description secondary. Nonetheless, we hope that these brief narratives—through anecdotes, some occasional basic information, and historical facts—might enhance a reader's experience of the City of Hartford.

You can hold this book in your hands free from highway development, urban renewal, Six Pillars, and IQuilts. This is here. This is now. Forty-four diverse voices have spoken in the way that they speak. Hear what we've got to say. It's poetry, it's art. It does not claim to be perfect-in-planning or on the page. It's a 2024-time capsule for the Capital City of Connecticut—Hartford. In a short description of downtown Hartford from the *New York Times* of October 30, 2022, Rory Gale, the owner of Hartford Prints!, said the following regarding the city's potential: "There's always this great momentum, and then a decline, and then great momentum. We're always almost getting there." May this volume work as one small effort, one push to get us there—wherever that may turn out to be.

—Dennis Barone and Deborah Ducoff-Barone

The Poems

Bessy Reyna

Freedom Journeys in Four Voices

The extraordinary autobiography *Life of James Mars, A Slave Born and Sold in Connecticut* (1868) led me to the story of Nancy Jackson, the young slave woman granted her freedom in 1837, by the Supreme Court of Errors located at the Old State House. To this day, the case of *Jackson v. Bullock*, 12 Conn.38 (1837) is held as one of the most celebrated and far-reaching decisions because of its impact in ending slavery in Connecticut.

(Voice 1: Hardy)
At an early age I became a sentinel.
I protected a runaway slave hidden in the closet
inside my house at 27 Main Street, Farmington, Connecticut.
I sat, all day, on the front steps obeying my father's instructions
to stop anyone from entering, and not to answer their questions.

All alone, I confronted the slave hunter,
a red-faced Southern man who came frantically driving
his lather-covered horse down Main Street.
That day, I learned what it is to be an abolitionist
to give moments of kindness and dignity to runaway slaves.

I am **Mrs. Aaron Hardy**, and I did those things
when I was **Mary Ann Cowles**, little more than a child,
the courageous child has lived within me since.

(Voice 2: Downer)
My name is **Mary K. Downer**.
As a student in the Third prep class of 1855,
I posed this question on my essay: "Is it a sin to own slaves?"
I need to know. I am confused, pulled in two directions.
"A very beautiful and graceful paper" my teacher wrote.
I was not asking for her praise but for the truth.

(Voice 3: Jackson)
My name is **Nancy Jackson**.
My freedom will depend on the judges' interpretation
of the meaning of the word "Left."
This word being tossed around, turned over,
flattened, inflated and dissected by the Supreme Court.

(Voice 4: Mars)
My name is **James Mars**,
I was born a slave in Connecticut and I am not a hero.
I just had to help that young woman, Nancy Jackson.
Others helped me, and my family, when we ran away.
Like Mrs. Darby, who had so little to give but she took me in.
No one suspected a fugitive could hide in her one-room house.

(Downer)
In school I have been taught that "thousands of these unfortunate
people have been kidnapped from their native lands,
by white men professing Christianity."
In church, I hear that they have been
"torn from their friends taken to foreign countries,
sold into perpetual slavery, treated unmercifully."

(Jackson)
In court one lawyer asks if I was
"disposed of, held in bondage against the law?"
I am trying so hard to understand this legal talk.
Another says I was "Suffered to remain" in Connecticut.

The words sound pretty,
but it is the five judges' definition
of the word "left" that will decide my future.

(Downer)
What if? ... I asked in my essay
What if things were the other way around?
What if we, the Europeans, were the slaves,
and the Africans our masters?
How would we like to be torn away from our families
to be sold, humiliated, beaten.

(Mars)
The men who came to tell me about Nancy said:
Deacon James, we want to make a strike at liberty!
I liked the sound of that!
A strike at liberty, to erase a scar from the back of a slave,
like my grandmother who was tied and whipped
until her blood covered the ground.

(Jackson)
I tremble, I tremble hearing the lawyers say words I never heard before
like "Non-importation Law of 1774."
Was I imported in 1835, like the furniture the Bulloch family
brought with them?
Two years I lived in Hartford, caring for their daughters,
learning about the lives of free colored men and women
like Deacon Mars, who works at a shop, and his wife who
does laundry for the Bullochs.
I want to be like them. I won't go back to Georgia.

(Downer)
A white world, and a black one surround and separate me,
dividing my mind and my heart.
If "Man is the most perfect of all God's works,"
why is it that I am not allowed to know Africans
or to go to school with them?

(Mars)

No! We could not let that Presbyterian Elder James Bulloch
keep Nancy a slave.
We created an excitement like Hartford had never seen before.
Like all of Connecticut had never seen before!
The abolitionist Theodore Weld, and the lawyer, Mr. Ellsworth,
wrote a *Writ of Habeas Corpus*
because Nancy had been "illegally confined for a long time."
I was so proud when I signed that application to the Court.

(Downer)

The teacher tells us that in our country there are many
slaves separated from everyone they love.
Poor wretches wishing they were in their graves.
In church, and in school, we repeat and repeat
"Man is the most perfect of all God's works,"
but is not a slave also a man?
I must believe it is a sin to own slaves.
I most certainly do believe it is a great sin.

(Mars)

Yes, I was proud to help Nancy, but during those ten days till the
    decision
I saw the hold slavery had on the feelings of Hartford people.
I was frowned upon, blamed, told I had done wrong, I should be
    mobbed.
That the house where I live should be pulled down,
all this, by men of wealth and standing.

(Jackson)

Two of the judges would send me back to slavery.
Two were for my release.
Am I standing at the threshold of my freedom, or my death?
We shall hear Chief Judge Williams with the final vote
of the Connecticut Supreme Court of Errors
    tomorrow at 8 o'clock.

I sit in court, waiting quietly, gently touching the two opium pills
I have sewn inside my pocket. It is my secret.
I will not go back even if the court orders me to.
I have been a slave my 24 years and I rather die!

(Narrator)

The room grew very quiet when Judge Williams spoke

"*In the case of Nancy Jackson v James Bulloch, it is the opinion
of a majority of the court, that this slave was brought and left in this state,
contrary to the act of 1774, and therefore, that she cannot be claimed
or treated as a slave under our laws. We therefore advise that she be
discharged.*"

(Jackson)

As I left the courthouse, surrounded and supported by my
lawyers, I whispered to myself: My name is **Nancy Jackson** and I belong
to no one!

Joan Hofmann

Beech Tree in the Garden of the Butler-McCook House

I'm drawn to touch the greyed trunk
of the tall beech, to circle my hands
over its flat round face, thin as drum skin.
I look up into the massive canopy
urging me to climb onto snaked limbs
into its tangled embrace.

I remember at twelve years, clutching
a beech like this while knifing names
inside carved hearts, forever-loves.
Giddy girls with meager knowledge
of the young boys we paired with
in daydreams. We told stories sitting
in the crooks of The Carving Tree
whose smooth skin held our initials
together with etched arrows angled
like clasps.

Then, we didn't know we held
but a crude view of connection—such
naiveté about being one and partnering
as two. Now, I memorize the arms of
inosculated branches above me: a dream
of confluence, limbs draped over winded ones
rubbed raw, conjoined cambium layers grown
together into a nettle of temper, settled,
like two resting in each other's arms.

I imagine a couple's evolved ways,
each the other's best thing. Embarrass

yourself and it's no matter, not noticed—
a laying on of hands, without religion
or heresy, like listening to corn grow or
comforting someone alone in hospital to
be free from fear: *What if no one comes for me?*

I've sat under this beech before,
not regretting marriage, but aching
its failure. In my life I've loved and
been loved in the safe nest of partnership,
touched its boundaries and depth. I've
known the why and extent of pairing,
its potency and fragility, its organicity.

We can possess and be possessed like
lichen's fungus and algae, composite
with each other yet self-affirming.
I admire longevity with its beauty
of worn down and grown into.
I want the mutuality of the oxpecker
on the rhino's back, how a fig tree
depends on, must have, the fig moth.

Frederick-Douglas Knowles II

Blood-ink

from *Frederick Douglas: Prophet of Freedom*

Frederick,

may I call you   Frederick   Mr. Douglas?
I never knew   the spine   of this church

we fused   63,177 days   apart
was instituted   by a Hooker?

-Thomas Hooker,

the minister   who fore-fathered   an exodus
from   Cambridge   to Hartford,

the city   that misplaced my Nanna's birthdate,

where a mob   cast you   from a hall,
tatted   your abolitionary dress   in eggs

hatching   *nigger*   from callous   shells
        as if its   inhumanity

            were laid by fowl.

Your suasion   sanctuary-less   until
this   church   Center Church   cleansed

your quill   *under open sky*   story-lining
from your   "makeshift soapbox"   that

prejudice against color was rebellion against God.

I never knew   ambling   into the   arms
of this church   that you   ancestrally

shouldered me   from shells   173 years   earlier.
That   my poems   were pages   in a plot

where   blood-ink eyes   etch your name
in the annals   of a city   you were sent to save.

Sally Van Doren

A Visit to the Wadsworth

First, to find the front door
among the five forbidding facades.
Is it a castle, a church, a fortress—
another insurance company HQ?
No, it's an atheneum, a cultural
center devoted to the arts, built
with granite, marble, concrete,
glass and steel to bolster
the creative spirits it houses.
Fortunately, there's a sign
that says "Enter Here."
Each step up the rough-hewn stones
brings us closer to monumentality.
It's not a square or a rectangle,
but a many-sided mausoleum
where paintings and sculptures
are preserved for the ages.

Our heads bow under the darkened
Gothic archways. They make us
pause and think. We're bound
by Prospect Street and Main.
We ponder both our future and
our past. We can mix Beaux-arts
and neo-Brutalism and still be
whole. All our geometries are
welcome. Inside the Great Hall,
the light pours in through
clerestory windows and rounded
vaults. Circles and majestic
semi-circles soften the angles
of the walls peopled with old masters

in gilded frames. Humbled and in awe
we exit left and climb the oval staircase
to see more art, to take our part.

Chase Twichell

Church Ghosts

Asylum Hill Congregational Church

What a beautiful dinosaur, the church!
Its ruckled brownstone hide
has settled on the excellent
posture of its bones.
It has eaten well, and is calm.
In its head is an eye that tells time.
It has studied our comings and goings
for one hundred and fifty years.
The eye can see the original Asylum
where the deaf and dumb
were taught to translate silence.
Later they changed its name
from Asylum to School.
Drawn by the stained-glass hymns,
their ghosts still visit, appearing
and disappearing at all hours,
loitering outside
the closed blue doors.

Brian Johnson

Colt's World

Yes, the Colt complex,
All of Coltsville.

To be part of it,
The complex, this history
Of guns and money
In Connecticut.

And the royal blue onion:
Is it Slavic? Islamic?
Quite incongruous – the colt too,
The prancing colt.

Dome, colt,
Fancy that.

And touring the complex:
How is it that all these windows,
These gun-making machines,
Are still intact?

There are signs of life
At the old factory;
Some efforts at renovation,
And nearby, the workers' cottages—

This is the frontier birthplace,
The origin story of guns
In the late morning sun
Of a national park.

Anita Durkin

Squirrel in a House Museum

Eighteen claws thin as burgeoning roots
On the oak he vaults from. Lion's paws
On chairs behind the walls he hollows
His home inside. Squirrel is no

Stone sentry on a library; he's the scrape
Of whittled joists, feet no bigger
Than a bulb that clasp the bark to halt
Mid-leap. We preserve to remember.

Possessions replace the woman who wrote
Inside. Red velvet Louis Quinze
For the sixty, seventy, eighty-something
Body too light to leave an impression

In its cushion. We never build fires,
Though by the mantle the scent of smoke sometimes
Comes through, the tap of Squirrel's scurry echoes
Off the tiles. Where no one lives, he is

Unwelcome. The skeletal remains
Of abandoned structures are no more his
Domain than the empty places within
The walls, where we can't fit

Without a crowbar, where we can't extract
Him without carving out space enough
For ourselves. And the Director of Collections roots
For the hawk roosting on the eaves.

Antoinette Brim-Bell

Song for the Talcott Street Congregational Church

Praise this church that cradled to its bosom
the palpitating hearts of the fleeing.
Doors flung wide; door jambs
set strong as deliberate sentries.
Praise casements swung open to unclouded skies,
windows sealed against despairing rains.
Blessed be the righteous soles that stood
on floorboards hewn by hand, polished with beeswax
and oil by tired women on bended knee.
Glory be this church of underground secrets,
its rafters swollen with prayer. Praise be the pulpit—
the Bible set by a benevolent hand—
this man bold enough to reclaim his own soul.
Bless the congregation wrapped in threadbare sackcloth.
Sing for those who could be men within these walls,
and the children free to dream there.

Ginny Lowe Connors

The Mark Twain House

Piloting a steamboat along the Mississippi—
ah, those were the days. Pull up a chair and he'll tell
you one story after another of his life on the river.
He's settled down now. More or less.

So then this house. To hold the stories, hold his family close,
hold him up as a man of means. Man of accomplishment.
His house stately as a steamboat, plowing through Hartford's
rumpled air. Red brick and splash. Gaudy and gabled.

A restless traveler, Sam adores the exotic.
His home's entryway is a Turkish bazaar. Plush carpets,
oriental vases, exotic stencils, rich carvings.
A barefoot boy travelled a long way. He said, *I have arrived.*

The family's cats become lions and tigers stalking
and pouncing in the conservatory—a jungle of green.
Sunlight dazzles the rubber plants. Is it fountain or waterfall
that burbles and cascades? Every day the place must be tamed again.

Sometimes Sam himself is the jungle cat, and little Jean rides him
into the library. This room's another story that three little girls demand.
A whisper, sudden exclamation, a mystery, a warning.
Start with the cat in a ruff and include all items on the mantle.

Within this boisterous household, the master bedroom
is a benediction. Cherubs emerge from a bed
elaborate with carvings. Pillows go at the foot of the bed
so Sam and Livy's drowsy eyes can gaze upon angels before sleep.

Cigar smoke and whiskey mark the billiard room.
Friday nights, friends gather, knock balls across green felt,
tell tall tales, turn the air blue. Most days, Sam hunches
over the corner desk. Scribbling, reflecting, crossing out.

Tom, Huck and Jim live here, and a prince, a pauper.
Ghosts of them still roam the Twain house,
though the family is gone. A Connecticut Yankee
peers out the window, betting on an eclipse.

The rags of love remain. Walls listen as Sam swears
at a new-fangled gadget, the telephone. Livy
clucks her tongue. Baby Langdon reaches out
his chubby arms. That moaning may be the wind.

It may be Susy, delirious with meningitis. Brilliant girl
full of fire, full of plans. How alone she is at the end.
Fortune and catastrophe, sorrow and celebration
find each other here. As in any great story.

Catherine E. Hoyser

Miss Lucy Barbour's School for Girls

Tucked away from prying eyes,
modest as females should be, girls
recited: I am/you are/she/he/it is

sun-dulled brick moss fringed
from once sapling oaks that stretch
sunward over 100 years. Crumbled

pointing lets mice squeeze into its winter
warmth. The double doorway's steps
dip from so much to-ing and fro-ing.

White ruffled pinafores over rough Prussian
blue wool dresses striate the white chalk
paint on the walls when the girls march

to class. Warped walnut floors, made
from Sam Clemens's lumber leftovers,
continue to make tables tilt. Purple paint

drops sunk into floor crevasses during
banner making—Votes for Women—no
one notices. Once whole now

chopped into three homes, energy
zigzags where once female power
flowed straight like tree trunks. Listen

closely for the recitations; taste
their cabbage soup lunch; smell
the beeswax; squint in the gaslight

to read McGuffey—I was, you were,
he/she/it was.

Tom Nicotera

Charter Oak Cultural Center

Outside
(A View from South Prospect Street)

Easy Shopping Grocery Store,
Capital Spirits Beer, Wine, Liquor,
a red brick triplex rowhouse,
and then there it rises,
a temple turned cultural center,
majestic with its impressive frame,
its twin wide circular towers,
its contrasting colors of red brick
and green window frames,
its brown tiled roofs (four roofs
if you count the two towers
and the small rectangle of a dormer
facing forward between the towers).
The twin doors are arched
as are most of the windows
except one small graceful window
with a circular center and eight small circles
radiating out from its center,
looking like a stemless green flower
in the prime of summer.

Spires top the towers
and the main gabled roof features
a prominent weather vane
probably doubling as a lightning rod.
Cast iron railings lead to the front doors
and above the doors large gold letters state
"Charter Oak Cultural Center."

Inside

Once inside the synagogue,
there is a sense of awe, not only as a place of worship,
but as a place of history. Dating from the 19th century,
it's the oldest synagogue in Connecticut.
It then became a Baptist church.
It has the original design
by well-known architect George Keller—
from the wooden pews, with arches
carved in at both ends, to the gigantic wooden
arches supporting the ceiling beams.
On both sides of the interior, large arches,
perpendicular to each other, hover over the side aisles
alongside the pews. And carved into these arches,
which appear suspended from ceiling beams,
are smaller circles and three-ring clover shapes
(with a triangle carved here and there).
Overall, there is an aura of the mysteries of geometry.

Gradually descending, the pews face a small space
where the altar would have been. Upraised
about two feet from the floor, it now looks
like a small stage. Another arch frames this space,
and on the back wall, about fifteen feet high
is another arch, a stained-glass window actually,
with that same eight-petaled flower shape
I saw on the building's outside.
But now with a closer look, I can see
the splendor of its details: rectangles
radiating out from the center
which is a white tablet of scripture.
Around the tablet are two concentric circles
in red and orange, bisected by eight rectangles
leading to the intersections of the eight glass arches,
thus giving the uniformity of appearance

of a flower and its petals. Within these small arches
are smaller shapes—ellipses, triangles, lines.
Surrounding this giant flower-looking design
are smaller floral shapes and triangles enclosing circles,
and circles within circles. Again, here are the mysteries
of geometry--equilibrium, parallelism and, ultimately,
balance. To be surrounded by such perfection
induces wonder and peace.

Finally, stained glass windows line both sides of the temple.
Tall arches frame the windows, and the glass forms
arches within these arches, and these windowed arches,
decorated in blue, gold and white with floral designs,
frame a cross-work of squares and triangles,
depending on how you look at them.
Once again, the contours of mathematics
inspire harmony, wonder, beauty.
And the translation of the scripture
above the altar in that window?
"Know Before Whom You Stand."

As I leave, I look back at those words above the door,
"Charter Oak Cultural Center,"
a one-time Jewish temple,
a center of faith and prayer, a center for God,
now a center for art and culture,
a temple in its own way
for the believers in expression,
the commonality of our many evocations
of the human race, both believers in God
and nonbelievers, for all are welcome
to the galleries, concerts, poetry readings,
changing exhibits and community outreach programs,
welcome to pay attention, be moved, feel hope,
and yes, even pray at what may inspire them,
here at a temple in more ways than one,

a seeming anomaly in this city space
with an enormous apartment building
as two folded wings behind it,
this paeon to history,
this ode to the arts,
this promenade of culture,
this testament to the human spirit.

Steve Straight

The Richardson Building (built 1875-1876)

Designed by Henry Hobson Richardson
Commissioned by Rush and Frank Cheney

Legend has it that a Chinese princess discovered silk
when a cocoon fell out of a tree and into her tea. The hot tea
dissolved the hard gum and allowed the princess to
unravel the cocoon as a single strand.

On my way into the brewery
I stop before I reach the red awning,
rest my hand on the Portland brownstone
quarried from just down the river in 1875,
gaze at the five giant arches forming the first two floors
with their alternating bricks of white Berea limestone,
then up at the smaller arches above them, 2-6-2 across,
and still higher as the motif repeats again, 3-14-3,
and then over all the vault of sky.

Inside, no more dry goods, no more linens,
muslins, shawls, or notions, and no silk in sight.
No more Brown, Thomson or G. Fox,
no more afternoon tea in the cafeteria
with its crustless sandwiches of cream cheese and salmon.
Instead I am greeted by giant copper kettles and tanks,
their temperature controlled by the steady city steam
that flows underground.

From a snug under the chandelier that might be Tiffany,
ringed with marble angels at the top,
the view of the arched window is even more dramatic.
This is the stuff of architects, of course,
Richardson and his homage to the Romanesque,
plus the men who commissioned him,
two of five Cheney brothers from my hometown,

inventors and tinkerers in Manchester's silk mills
whose Rexford Roller revolutionized silk production,
not to mention the workmen and artisans,
Italians and Irish and Germans,
fitting wedge-shaped *voussoirs*
into the sweeping symmetry of brick and glass,
gargoyles between the arches.

As the head subsides on my City Steam IPA,
orange twilight streaming through the magnificent arches,
I can't help thinking of the smallest artisan,
who paid for all this, *Bombyx mori*, the silkworm,
which spins its cocoon by rotating its body
in a figure-8 three hundred thousand times,
the single strand more than 1000 yards long.
Like the princess, we still extract the silk by boiling the cocoons,
our tiny artisans becoming the dregs of their own tea.

John L. Stanizzi

Finding St. Anthony

Learn to love humility, for it will cover all your sins. All sins are repulsive before God, but the most repulsive of all is pride of the heart.
—St. Anthony the Great

1. The Past

Changes fled past, wraiths of history,
shades of what was. *St Paul's Episcopal* sold
to the *German Lutheran Church of Reformation*,
beaten by weather and use, bearing grief's hue of dusk.
1898, Lutherans sold the building to a church in waiting—
St. Anthony's Roman Catholic, ready to aid
the spiritual needs of Faithful Italian Americans.
The Hartford diocese founded St. Anthony's
on Front Street, a derelict neighborhood, unstable
on the tightrope between "neighborhood" and "slum."
Most of the apartments' foundations crumbled,
blown away by filthy wind, degrading tenants.
Nana and Grampy lived there with 9 children—
7 boys, 2 girls, in a two-bedroom apartment
the size of a hope chest. Grampy and Nana
had one bedroom. Emmanuella & Carmella, the other.
The 7 boys? How can one articulate so dreadful a thing?
Across the street the immense river, epic sidewinder,
slinked in silence, pit organ always ready.
The tumbledown apartments on Front Street
leaned and shook, bristling with people starved for room.
Front Street, exposed, sat head-on in the sights
of the huge river. Talcott Street, St. Anthony's new home,
would be plagued by a river engorged, coming in high
and hard, wind baying savage strike screeches.
Precious St. Anthony's, which many held *sanctified*,
was about to be taken. Everything in the path

of the enraged river was smashed and splintered.
A squall, impossibly strong, roared into that *Holy Place*,
the church where members trusted their most intimate secrets.
That little basilica destroyed by what had become
a vast channel decimating "Little Italy."
This disaster was not the end for the embattled poor.
The next maelstrom's vicious crash would be
just two years later. *The Great New England Hurricane*
of 1938. It hit relentlessly. Everything that had
been destroyed in 1936 was violated again,
prompting an immediate move out of there.
St. Anthony's went to cobblestoned Morgan Street,
then Market Street, and finally, Church Street.
Hartford's politicians deemed "Little Italy" a slum,
and soon Connie and Diane would finish her off.
Connecticut was lashed with 13 to 20 inches of rain
between August 11 & 13. Connie blasted through first.
Diane finished the job. 87 dead. Over $350 million
dollars damage. What the future held for Front Street
couldn't be imagined. It would come from a distant future.
Front Street had succumbed.

2. The Future

*St, Anthony, venerated worldwide as the patron saint of recovering
things lost—including lost people …*

In the early 1950s when I was a damaged child
sent to live with Zia Rosa, I played under the maples
lining Albany Avenue. The pigeons would come so close
I might have held one. Across town where Grampy and Nana
had lived, their tiny world changed so horribly fast
they were beaten into sickened confusion.
Apartments, like the "forts" kids made, had once lined
Front Street, but they were being razed and all that remained

were ditches filled with corpses of memories piled stiff,
one on top of the other, rats fleeing the land they defiled.
Giovanirro Stanizzi and *Felicia DeCorleto*,
my parents, were married in 1947 at St. Anthony's
with its ferocious history of floods and fires. St. Anthony's,
now on Church Street, where my parents were married
in a little basement chapel. One grainy photo
of the wedding party remains, everyone posing
on *large stone steps*. I didn't learn until recently
that the photo was *not* taken at St. Anthony's.
My mother explained that St. Anthony's didn't have
any large stone steps. St. Anthony's didn't have *any* steps.
But on that joyous day, high spirits were not
to be trifled with. The whole wedding party traveled to
the Beneventis, friends of my parents. Their building
had beautiful stone steps, the steps where
the iconic photo was taken—
the *stand-in* for their beloved St. Anthony's.
But soon there came a darkness, a rift which
shredded our family. I have no details, I just know that
my father's siblings, and all my cousins, disappeared
like smoke into the coming years.
1958—St. Anthony's & St. Patrick's merged. I was nine.
This was now *my* church. Its motto—
"Open hearts, Open minds, Open doors."
At Mass one Sunday, with Big Millie & Little Millie,
something mystifying occurred. Father was just
beginning the Liturgy of the Eucharist when *shock struck!*
I knew no one in this church—no one! But it happened!
Someone behind us whispered loudly,
STANIZZI! HEY! STANIZZI!
I turned to look—*more shock!* There was my cousin Sonny!
I hadn't seen him in a very long time. I missed him terribly.
When Mass was over, I walked out, hiding between
Big and Little. I should have run to him, but I had no words,
and what if he didn't know me? But here he was!

Thank you! Oh, thank you so much for finding Sonny,
Dear St. Anthony. Sonny, who slipped away one day
long ago, into the multitudes, and today he slipped
right back in ... perfectly. Give thanks.

Maria Sassi

One Dawn, Fast-Walking in Hartford

My sneakers whacking the sidewalk block
by block, city air settled, almost sweet
as it carried the wail of the 6 a.m. down
from Boston. That sound. Clemens, way back,
heard it whistling over the mist of little
Hog River that ran by his house. He would
be out there on his filigreed veranda
observing the sky, pull out his watch at
the train's call, then slap the rail of his
veranda and go walking down his river boat
deck. It rolled beneath him . . .

Harmonic wail, half mournful, half enticing—
Stevens heard it sorrowing over the sleeping
houses, into his screened window, ruffling
his papers, his poems as he packed a briefcase
for the long walk to his office near the Capitol.
Walking east, he could see how a rising sun creates
various scintillations on the gold of the dome
and may have stopped to scrawl a word, a line,
then go on . . .

The men who first layered the leaves of gold
on the Capitol dome were up there by dawn
and the wail of the 6 a.m. was faint and far
as they practiced their jeweler's art in the sky—
always wishing to work safe hours before
bright sun created gleamings, a sparkling
on gold that unsettled their footing, their sight.
I heard how years later some had bad dreams—
walls of sun, eyes burning, a slip on a curve,
scaffold breaking like tulip stems and falling

around them as they walked down air,
the bright noon air . . .

Benjamin S. Grossberg

The Soldiers and Sailors Memorial Arch

Two brownstone Rapunzel towers connected
by an arch—

but under the two witch's-hat domes, no
Let down your hair to me.

Yet one can blink the metal gridding
off the high windows
and place there, instead, a blond-headed princess
leaning out, uncoiling in moonlight
the twin ropes of her hair.
Or make that *two* princesses, one in each tower,
feeding braids down stone intentionally left rough,
lowering them past the frieze
(in contrasting white stone, a tumble of calvary)

as, from the crenelated bridge,
a pair of princes strides up, all satin and swagger
and satin and swagger, chanting *Rapunzel, Rapunzel,*

and somewhere inside, behind the slats
of locked oak doors, two witches sleep—
stirring only a little when princes' footfalls
beat against their chambers' outer walls.

Those walls read (again, in white stone):

IN MEMORY OF THOSE WHO FELL
ON LAND AND ON SEA.

But how little it takes
to glimpse in the arch something fantastical—

to imagine a yellow pennant atop each tower,
five ruffed men blowing long brass horns,
and an Elizabeth in ermine walking beneath,
her right hand raised, crowds cheering for her…

and also, once a year, for us
as we pass under it after twenty-six miles,
a series of foam mats and (taped between them)
the wire that clicks in our time
as the MC announces it, along with our names.

Spectators line the approach,
some of them ringing bells, and volunteers
hand us a water bottle, drape on our shoulders
our own cape—reflective foil
to hold heat—and place around our necks
the finisher's medal,
the arch now a door from exhaustion and pain
to an earned euphoria.

On each side, just under the ring of windows,
the soles of his boots against cold stone,
a prince extends a hand,
and a princess grabs it
hurriedly drawing him inside; below,

snoring witches dream of plump children
and the tang of red berries
that would poison any other living thing;

and underneath, a stately queen, five long
horns blaring, and cheering bells
as runner after runner
                              passes through:

we have trained so hard. Our toenails
have blackened, our toes bled.
We have become—over months of training—
obsessed. And we get, under the arch,
our own fairy-tale ending.

Asia Hamilton

Hartford's Union Station

After the voyages of horse-drawn
Carriages, a massive creation
Erected—today's well-known
Union Station. Its intricacies, formed
With vigor of iron and brass,

Outshine the Park River. After the 1914 fire
New renovations transpired.
Bus and rail travel hassle-free.
Many sided, many faces
Multi-User restoration

Additions like CTTRANSIT and CTRAIL
Help us move in impressive array.
An anchor for travel that we must protect,
Hartford's Union Station,
Center to this great Historic Place.

Sean Frederick Forbes

Photo Shoot

The Linden
June 21, 2023

My former student turned photographer
and I are walking south on Main Street.

We're in search of buildings with distinctive
exterior features and textures, varying

backdrops for my professional headshots.
Kayla's pupils enlarge: red sandstone, brick,

a grand oxidized cupola; artistic architecture
built in 1891. I tell her I toured a condo

in this building once with my best friend Dina
about fourteen years ago. A junior attorney

at a prominent Hartford law firm, and living
in the city's historic district was next level:

paraquet hardwood floors, snug, yet inviting galley
kitchen, exposed red-brick walls— "rooms large

enough for comfort, and are small enough to look
cozy and be easily furnished," notes an article

in the *Hartford Courant* from January 1892. We'd
daydream about dinner parties she'd host, being

invited to happy hours, networking events by other
bright, young attorneys, doctors, educators at Hartford's

first luxury apartment house; the comforts of home set
against the backdrop of a unique urban neighborhood.

Kayla and I approach the massive curved corner
of the building. I tell her Dina had made a solid offer

that wasn't accepted, we both state "too bad" in near unison,
we avert our gazes to the steady rows of windows lined

in rhythmic fashion, passageways for passersby
to imagine the interior cherry birch woodwork.

I've mused for too long; Kayla suggests we walk to other
city landmarks since we've only another hour left to the session.

I take quick shots of the rock-faced masonry
that appears on the window lintels and sills,

of the doors painted black with a dull matte sheen,
the quaint sign that reads "1 Linden Place," a building

whose rough-faced stature attracts the attention of all
who pass along the street.

Brad Davis

Over On Woodland

In San Damiano, a stone chapel, nothing florid, no windows.
In San Francisco, a world-class yacht club.
Here in Hartford, over on Woodland, a hospital.

Likely there's a Saint Francis near you.
Maybe you were confirmed in Saint Francis Church.
Maybe you grew up on Saint Francis Street.

Among the saints my Catholic schoolmates knew
the way I knew players from baseball cards,
Francis was the only one I cared about.

I loved how he loved animals. Like the mangy cats
I kept bringing home to be received
about as well as homeless women would be

at that San Francisco yacht club—a club I know only
from a wedding reception there and how
the happy couple sailed off on a sixty-foot Oyster.

But in San Damiano, Francis wept. A wooden cross
askew and teetering atop a dilapidated chapel.
Then that voiceless Voice directing, *Rebuild my house,*

beginning with the little ruin right before you.
Concern for little things, like my wife's knee, bone
on bone, I take as divine. How Francis worked, stone on stone.

So no surprise, the choice between Hartford hospitals
was never in doubt. And her best memory
of the ordeal bears out the wisdom of her choice.

It is of Ruiz, a brown-skinned man in a golf cart.
He drove her to the elevator in Saint Francis
for ascending to the hospital's joint replacement institute,

then, grinning, pledged to pray for her recovery.
An outward, unexpected sign of an inward,
unaffected *yes* she was glad to welcome. And of course

when Dennis Connor or any sailing Hall of Famer,
their shiny, world-class honors on display
in the yacht club's artful rows of well-surveilled cases,

needs a knee replaced, they don't reserve a table
in the club's Clipper Ship or Race Deck or Main Dining Room.
They want what that world cannot give and she received.

Julien Strong

At Keney Clock Tower

The instructions in his will said to erect it
as a memorial to his grocery business
that once stood on this site.
But the plaque in the tower's shadow says

it was erected to the memory of
"the wisdom, goodness, and womanly nobility"
of Henry Keney's mom.

Like something stolen from a gothic fortress,
the imposing blocks of brown sandstone
are relieved only by high vertical slits
as through which an archer might aim

and shoot at the invading hordes
of abandoned buildings encroaching all around.
Gargoyles snarl at you from the tower's crown

while four iron faces of clocks
keep time on each side,
their hands all synchronized with one another
like people who have got their story straight—

who to love, what to honor,
how to leave a record of their lives
after they've gone. And yet

a man plans a memorial to himself,
someone else builds that memorial
to his mother, and time builds a memorial to
what happens in the gap between intent

and execution. You run your fingers
down the roughened stone, think about families,
and check the tower's clocks against your own.

Dennis Barone

Perfect Six

History is the end of all things eternal.
The a-historical bee never exits the hive.
We remember Achilles. Then recall that
He died. Sometimes we can glimpse
The pacing, the placing of our returns from
The theoretical to the autobiographical.
A door may open: the thing to do is enter.

Julia M. Paul

Connecticut Supreme Court Building

Set by itself, in all the majestic dignity which architecture can command, is rising before our eyes the splendid home which Connecticut has prepared for her highest court of justice...
—Former Chief Justice Simeon E. Baldwin, on laying the cornerstone, 1909

I

Individuals seeking to peaceably assemble during hours the building is open to the public may use a portion of the platform located in between the upper and lower steps at the front entrance of the Supreme Court building on Capitol Avenue.

II

Some say that justice dresses in suit and tie,
carries a leather briefcase with gold-embossed initials,
writes with a fountain pen. That sometimes justice
turns away from the impoverished, steps over the man
sleeping in the park, is beholden to the privileged.

III

Interpreting our state constitutional provisions ... leads inevitably to the conclusion that gay persons are entitled to marry the ... same sex partner of their choice. To decide otherwise would require us to apply one set of constitutional principles to gay persons and another to all others.
Kerrigan v. Comm'r. of Public Health, decided by the Connecticut Supreme Court, 2008

IV

Some say justice does not see itself in the faces
in the courtroom or feel the pinch of handcuffs
on those wrists. That justice is hard
as a marble stairway, as immovable as a stone pillar.

V

Public school children established prima facie showing that disparities in racial and ethnic composition of city public schools and surrounding communities ... jeopardized children's fundamental right to education ...
Sheff vs. O'Neill, decided by the Connecticut Supreme Court, 1996

VI

At street level, we tilt our heads back
to take in the portico at the top of thirty-seven wide steps.
School children on field trips enter here,
dwarfed by massive granite columns.
They tour the edifice of the Supreme Court,
point at the portraits of retired justices
and the mural behind the bench of the signing
of Connecticut's Fundamental Orders in 1638,
the first constitution in the United States.
Ryan, the future lawyer, tells his classmates,
"This is why we're the 'Constitution State.'"

VII

Every citizen may freely speak, write and publish his sentiments on all subjects...
Article first, §4, of the constitution of Connecticut

VIII

Some say justice speaks in ancient Latin—
res ipsa loquitor, caveat emptor, certiorari—
or worse, is silent. That heretofore and hereinbefore
are atrophying left and right arms
cloaked in the bat-wing sleeves of black robes.

VIX

It is the policy of the Connecticut Judicial Branch to accommodate individuals seeking to peaceably assemble outside of the Supreme Court Building.

X

A crowd gathers on the steps of the Supreme Court
to protest raids and arrests by agents of ICE in state courthouses.
Justice paces oak clad halls while chanting voices
slip through arched windows pleading to be heard.

XI

Inside, a teacher points out *the gilded ceiling mural* to her students,
explains that *the youths in the painting are moving forward*
guided by the Spirits of Wisdom and Progress as they
carry flaming torches representing the light of education,
and "See," she says, "how *the figures of Ignorance and Superstition*
are falling further into darkness as they're overpowered by that light."

Note: the italicized portions of the poem are taken from the CT Judicial
Website.

Kenneth DiMaggio

Ode to the G. Fox Department Store in Hartford

Large chrome
fluted Art Deco awning
above several revolving doors

not Macy's of New York City
but the former G. Fox department
store in Hartford

The 12-story sandpaper-textured
stone building home today
to a community college

Fifty years ago this large silver-
ware shiny tea tray-topped
entrance welcomed customers
in mink

Yes, remember the dignity
this grand dame once gave
to customers in furs

but share it with the students
struggling to become nurses
as they revolve through graceful
sculpted portals in their
baggy but still practical
scrubs

John Long

Travelers Tower, 360° View

#

Architecture is language.
A tower speaks to us—
we should ask the question:
is the company
making a statement?

#

1919: Travelers Insurance builds
the tallest building in Hartford
pushing higher
than all other companies
in the Insurance Capital,
reaching seventh highest
in the world.

#

It takes 10,000 tons
of pink granite,
4,200 tons of steel
for a tower
to convince us that
Travelers offers real protection
from catastrophes or financial ruin.
Its 2,000 windows
display the vision of business:
from above
in all directions,
locate opportunities
assess potential profit.

#

The Travelers first logo:
a suit of armor—
replaced by
a graphic of modern strength and grace:
the newly-built Tower.
Later it loses out to
a red umbrella.

#

1997: peregrine falcons,
madly in love,
build their nest on the tower
to produce three chicks.
Two years later
the peregrine falcon
is not an endangered species.
Wildlife, saved by this tower
rooted in city life.

#

Peregrine falcons dive
at 175 miles per hour,
to kill a pigeon in midair
and take it back to the nest.
The tower's height
is critical
to any efficient predator:
a clear view
of the bountiful food supply
in Bushnell Park,
then the launch.

#

What's the style?
Neoclassical, Beaux Arts, Renaissance Revival,
take your pick.
Each suggests tradition, financial wisdom.
Peregrine falcons prefer
ornamentation:
shapes in stone, uneven surfaces
for perches,
its cupola the perfect site
for their aerie.

#

Travelers Tower
is a monument
built on policy sales
filled with promises
(and provisos in fine print)
of safety, longevity, good health
for people and, as we now know,
peregrine falcons.

Richard Deming

Of Stevens and The Hartford in Morning Light

The hardest thing to imagine is him, the poet
of poets somewhere deep in that grand building

his portly frame, those shoulders, hunkered
across an oaken desk covered in ledgers, folders,

yellow legal pads. It doesn't add up. The tongue's
an eye, or so he wrote, and yet each day

his secretary tap-tap-typed out countless
contracts and memos, and if lucky

some lines the old man'd composed
as he walked to work. What did he think

as he strolled down Asylum Avenue, in the rain
or the snow or a heavy early sun until the Greek

columns of The Hartford loomed of a sudden
into his field of vision? We know or think

we do: word by word with each step
he muttered his poems like a sullen

blue jay settling along a greeny branch.
Then at last, a little out of breath, he ascended

those broad stairs to those wide doors
and pushed them aside, entering that space

to become some doubled self, some voice
caught between incantation and indemnity.

No matter what he asked of any
harried broker or distraught client,

this fractured life we all lead's
hardly sure nor assured, no matter

how high the ceilings or how gold
the arched dome vaulting above. That's

the fiction not to forgive, that nevertheless
begs belief and maybe he could insist

that happiness is an acquisition but still
the solid wall of The Hartford

never once hovered
against a too cruel New England sky.

Elizabeth Thomas

Falcon, 1997

i am a falcon
lord of the skies

I squeeze through the rowdy hallways
of Bulkeley High School,
searching for room 5.
It's my first day as a visiting poet
and I'm seriously questioning my mid-life
decision to switch careers.
Students who look old enough to be teachers
and teachers far younger than me,
scatter like Skittles in a maze of chaos.
Already, I feel dusty
as outdated as the books they carry.

fearless swift and mighty
a hunter like no other

Bravado fills these hallways,
spilling into classrooms
I have no business being inside.
I should be sitting in my corporate pod
in skirt and heels,
waiting for 3:10 to arrive.
Instead, I'm in jeans and a pair of Tims,
coffee cold in one hand,
sharp-tipped pencils
and paper overflowing my backpack.

that sweeps upon my prey

Friends shake their heads,
question my decision to start this new career.

Warn me to watch my back.
"Schools are not what they used to be,
you know."
And this, before school shootings
became so common.

but I'm also a piano
made of steel

I feel lost
in a tangle of bodies and breath,
cleavage and crop tops.
Yet, I believe this is what I was made for.
These kids, these blank pages, waiting
for their words.

strong and hard

Finally, I step inside room 5.
This is not a board room
of white men with receding hairlines
and hastily made-up women.
No corporate speak here.
"Hi, I'd like to talk about poetry,
how it saved my life."

but with a touch of the right key

And there he is—
back row
arms crossed, eyes angry
doesn't have a pen
doesn't want to borrow mine
doesn't want to be there.

i could become a soft symphony ~ Luiz

Susan Howe

from 118 Westerly Terrace

His alter ego "walked" —Henry James

Life in this house-island is

riddled with light a sense of

something last to say first

The tone of an oldest voice

Still one of great multitude

Afternoon at its most glassy

The foyer seems to smile

Who's down there with you
One and the selfsame giant
Sometimes bereft in quietness
he makes me as I meet him
grasp his arm—Going about
the house we enter the shade
of a careworn masterpiece

David Epstein

The Old Synagogue on Woodland Street

L'dor v'dor: liturgical Hebrew "From generation to generation"
Shul: Yiddish vernacular for synagogue, rhymes with school

Before it was a church,
the building was a *shul*,
the central dome as marigold
its purpose vertical.

The lives it has are in the stairs,
the treads as worn as stone,
where anyone who would ascend
assents to being gone

but not before the grasp of God
asserts in faithfully,
and brick by brick of ministry
collects the inter-awed.

Before it was a shul, the brick
was earthen lime and clay,
L'dor v'dor, in stone and skin,
all things pass this way.

And what about it gives it life?
Imagine it without:
a place where God anticipates,
who, certain, learns to doubt;

an emptiness where God awaits,
a sea, a fluke, a spout.

Charles Fort

Stage Light and the Arc of Human Color

1.

The city bus dropped me off at the library
I ran past the ancient graveyard and stone
garden scattered in the churchyard
into your arms past the sculptured swan.
Once young catching maple-helicopters
we held them at the end of the world.
Our eyes met in the sun-mad jazz festival.
After the carousel we walked to the arch
roundabout for war and fallen-soldiers.

2.

We were led by a ghost to our seats
inside the Bushnell Memorial Hall.
Marcel Marceau threw invisible arrows
captured inside his locked human cage
his hands turned into a tiny music box.
Alvin Ailey Dance Company, Pilobolus
We kissed in loge seats in our wrinkled jeans
front section private box of the first balcony
nearly heaven above the proscenium
the world made smaller into a larger stage.

3.

As a young lad I missed *James Brown and the Mighty Flames*
Please, Please, Please, Try Me, Please Don't Go, Lost Someone.
Hendrix set his guitar on fire, lighter fluid, matchbook
Voodoo Child (Slight Return). Purple Haze, Hey Joe

He made classical musicians wink in their sleep
compose the new melody set to constellations
before his Band of Gypsys ruled a burning world.

4.

Steppenwolf played *Magic Carpet Ride*
Goddamn the Pusher Man on Good Friday.
You lifted your veil and raised opera glasses
we found inside the fortune teller's tent.

My first plays at the Hartford Stage Company
Pinter's *Ashes to Ashes, A Kind of Alaska*
Years later I watched my youngest daughter
at Kenyon in the lead role as *Deborah*
in her senior recital of *A Kind of Alaska*.
Time and memory were falling embers.

5.

I was never seated next to Wallace Stevens
looking for symbols in The Petrified Forest
a stage-play and World Premiere of the film
Leslie Howard, Bette Davis, Humphrey Bogart
at Hartford's Parsons Theater Dec. 21, 1934?

The fortune teller told us we would be lovers
engaged in New Orleans wed in Connecticut
two daughters blessed in language and stage.
Had she known our future and not told us
I would become a widower twenty-one years
after being friends and lovers who met
under maple trees and swan-garden jazz?

6.

After the musician, actor, departed soldier
empty balcony seat, tangled shadow-mime
jazz and rock n' roll lost in the ember-cloud.
I ran back to the city bus inside a snow globe.
She had known our future and not told us.

Christine Beck

Hartford Public Library

They pose side-by-side—the Wadsworth Atheneum—
oldest art museum in the country, walls of massive
stone, housing art by Warhol and Picasso—
and the Hartford Public Library.

They doff their caps, two buildings with their pedigrees,
upholding Hartford's history, like pillars guarding
the entrance to a medieval city.

The library presents its huge glass window to the street,
where we cluster on its steps at 10am,
hug ourselves against the winter chill,
waiting like racehorses for the opening bell.

We rush inside, take up our positions
at the computer tables, wend our way
to classes on citizenship, how to get a GED,
the Civil War, or alternative medicine.

Weekdays, we grab a bite at the library's
coffee shop. Sundays, we tap our toes to
piano jazz in the performance space.

Three flights up, tucked in a corner,
is the Hartford History Room, no pens permitted,
documents under glass, white gloves required to handle them,
a history far removed from us downstairs.

We are living history, our dreams supported
with a myriad of programs and volunteers,
as we grow into ourselves, our stories part of history
in the rooms of the Hartford Public Library.

John Surowiecki

The Blue Buildings in the Summer Air

I

Crystalline buildings appeared one day
and new blue light poured through them.
The old neighborhoods vaporized in the glare.
That summer, the Roma settled in Hartford
handing out futures by the train station
and soon everyone was rich
and famous and desperately in love.

II

A new plaza returned the new light in blue waves.
A new cathedral grew out of a moss of familiar houses,
closer than anything else to the end of things.

In June we passed each other on the street,
a goofy kid and an obese poet in a gray suit.
The future was tidy and sequenced and sapphirine,
even for the poet whose end was a month or two away.

III

He imagined the offices inside the blue buildings,
cleared the desks of photos and knickknackery,

ordered lively posters in cold chrome frames—
a show of Mondrian's watercolors,
a look at Picasso during the war—

and there he was, drinking rare teas and talking into
a streamline Dictaphone with blinking blue lights.

IV

And the blue buildings had blue shadows which
children chased around the plaza.

There were blue lights at Christmas, too, self-
illuminating snow with Mozart in the air free of charge.

And the blue buildings were content to be moderately tall
and July-blue in July, the flimsiest of blues, recalling the skies
in places where crops were paid attention to.

V

Maybe he smiled at me as I walked by,
smiled and nodded as if to say he was
just an ordinary man living an ordinary life
in an extraordinary world where everyone

was an artist, no matter what, and here was where
that life began, in these buildings with blue skins
that blue light was passing through.

Sharon L. Charde

There Used to Be Music

for Saint Joseph Cathedral, 1956

So full of faith
in the unknown

I was shaped
by your shadows,

echoes of brown stone.
A girl in white

I approached
your altar, that long

aisle, slippery steps,
collected my prize,

kissed the ring,
sang mass, prayed

in your pews. You
taught me to stay

small, your dark
nave strange shelter

but shelter nonetheless.
After you burned, God

disappeared. I have lived
in the smoke for years.

James Finnegan

They Call It the Boat Building

—an elliptic lenticular cylinder

Is it a boat? I see it as an axe-blade—
"An axe against the frozen sea"
as Kafka described his work. Poised
against a sea of air stretching over
the Connecticut River all the way
to Long Island Sound. If it is a boat,
which end prow and which stern?

And then at certain times of day,
I think of Brancusi's "Bird in Space,"
and what if he had made a kind of fish,
and its windowpanes like fish-scales,
glistening as it cuts through,
not water, but another ether
that is the imagination loosed.

The company the building
was built for, is no more, assets sold,
the Phoenix Insurance Company
will not gather feathers enough
from a sunset's flames to rise,
as dusk settles in ash around it,
this boat, this bird, this fish, an axe.

Margaret Gibson

Beneath Cloud-Light

at the Unitarian Church in Hartford, Connecticut

Beneath cloud-light,
it's almost revelation to see a building as sculpted,

whose roof etches its fins against the sky as if supporting an upward
swoop of dolphins,
     or a rising-steadily-upward

silhouette of sharp-edged sea birds soaring wing by wing—

although the dissenter in me, the one embarrassed by so much
passion
    architecturally displayed in broad daylight,

might beg to differ; might, in a murmur,

ask if I'm looking at a circus tent of trapeze-like risings
and fallings—
     because, and oh, yes,

there's no one way to swoop upward and, simultaneously, not
leave the ground,

not just one pathway to God—

God a word for winged annunciations that open the heart,
so that this building—the rooted swoop of it—

becomes a visual definition that shows itself
in silence

and asks of us, in response, something like
prayer:

Let us be with whatever it is swoops us inward, outward, into
the company
of others,
            whispering

may we rise, may we all rise together.

Donna Fleischer

Bushnell Tower Plaza Fountain Sequential

July downtown hubbub
workers, sun splurged
break for lunch 'neath

tower rectangle
in trapezoid plaza with
fountain of circles

blackish slate tile
staggers another
tilted for

rainfall from cloud &
snaked rubber hose
emulating

flow into
round basin
within

ancient east
Asian landscape
bonsai 'round

sparse scrub pine,
sheared brown rocks on
end mountain-like jut

water sheet-like
unfolding into
water sheet-like

spilling over ledge
small birds, wings akimbo
how they hop they splash

'midst chalk-like
walkways, parking spaces
to and fro

upended rectangle
offsets frozen fountain
snow-ploughed plaza

mountains and rivers
far back cataract
beginning-less

simple module
repeatable rises
to 27 stories

reinforced
concrete pour,
girder, and pile

near Little River bedrock
western hill sloped
Bushnell Park neighbor

amassed
smooth cool quiet color
of sandstone

highest windows
pond light
ply sky, dew

sun cloud, bulb,
eyeball, observed
telescopic

so minimal as to
be almost caverned
blank without

message, adornment,
or symbol
to interrupt

the nothing
to read into so
something really lived in

since 1969
bees stirring in blue
people looking up

Ciaran Berry

Prince Rogers Nelson Live at the Albert C. Jacobs Life Sciences Center

I was there the day he passed away—accidental overdose, elevator,
    you'll remember. I was full of middle-aged dismay at these kids who
don't know their "Little Red Corvette" from their "Raspberry Beret,"

    though they school me on Bitcoin and Beyoncé, on Instagram, K-pop,
and Spotify. We were reading a poem by Natasha Trethewey based
    on a sketch by J.H. Hasselhorst in which a man dissects the body

of a suicide in order, the title suggests, to determine the ideal female
    form. Even now, he's drawing back the skin from her breastbone
as three other men look on, one bent over the face of the dead girl

    as if he's offering a lecture on anatomy, one the perfect emblem
of inquiry and erudition, right hand on hip, left scratching his chin.
    Science, which in 1864, is this skull split like a coconut and that

skeleton's ghost bones. Science, which, a hundred years later almost,
    sets up home in this brutalist edifice named for the college president
who placed a letter to the future at the cornerstone. In it he bemoans

    a "puzzling and dismal war" and "the problem of race and civil rights,"
something Trethewey locates in the Enlightenment, and the shape
    of these ever so learned men. We talk phrenology and ekphrasis

and what they got up to at the weekend until even the best students
    succumb again to the allure of their iPhones. A yellow glow rises
from between knees like the glow over the body in the chalk sketch

I project onto a drop screen, or the glow that follows his purpleness
as he exits stage left, leaving us bereft in the dry ice and holy smoke.
    Once, he wrote a fan letter to Joni Mitchell. Once, he called cellphones

"dismal gadgets." According to the coroner's report, what he thought
    was Vicodin turned out to be fentanyl—a problem we might add
to a list of what ails us in our response to Albert C. Jacobs, the gist

    of it that war has never gone away, and those red lines remain clear
as the stucco and steel girders in a style of architecture inspired
    by the high ideals of Le Corbusier, or the lines in this poem that,

against the best advice of Billy Collins, we tie to a chair and beat
    with a rubber hose. As Prince wrote, sometimes in April, it snows,
though how would we know in this classroom without windows?

    I loved him most singing "Kiss" in falsetto or, with "Darling Nikki,"
upsetting Tipper Gore. This must have been after and not before
    he fell head over high heels for Jehovah. Imagine him showing up

at your door with a copy of *The Watchtower* and the bass player
    from Sly & the Family Stone. Imagine him, live from this life sciences
center, entering the outro to "Purple Rain" on his symbol shaped guitar.

Marilyn E. Johnston

Reflecting in Hartford's Gold Building

When they hung glass up
on all sides of the building,
like gold-leaf's gold-tinted water,
divided into grids

you became my mirror, reflecting
my ever-hanging lines
                    of wash, shingled
roofline, church cupola detached and floating
in a square all its own,
                    my windows dark splinters
walking out of your edge.

Which is the real surface?
                I'm torn to shreds
in how you receive me
in your glass castle eyes
                Gold Building

It's what I see
off your sides dims me.
For you, I'm thin as abstraction
sliding off. I have no reality

in blue and golden sky
pink-edged clouds.
While my stolid world
scores of heavy lives in each ripple
wobble in and out mid-air.

Who was I before you stepped in?
Why can't I take my eyes
off your gold, glimmering stories.

Daniel Donaghy

Dancing with Abigail to "So Young and in Love"

Hartford's XL Center, 2/28/08

I took my daughter to see Bruce & the E Street Band at the XL Center—
last time Big Man, Clarence Clemons, blew his sax at the XL Center—

6'5", 240—*too fucking big to die*, Bruce said in his eulogy—but he did,
a few years after his opening riff split the panting dark of the XL Center

before a spotlight found Bruce spinning around his mic stand,
scatting lyrics to a super-deep cut from '78, the year the XL Center

roof collapsed under a foot of January snow, three years after it opened
with the promise of drawing more money downtown. The XL Center

rose from written-off lives, from shuttered shops imploded
between Trumbull, Ann Uccello, Church, and Asylum. The XL Center:

sixteen thousand silent seats waiting for a circus or band
that needs a gig between Boston and New York. The XL Center:

just a shell until there's a moment to live in. When Bruce screamed
Is anybody alive out there? We shouted back *Yes,* the XL Center

a riverside revival, a communion of souls. When he asked
it again—carnival barker, itinerant huckster—the XL Center

screamed back louder: older fans like me recalling their dead,
kids like my ear-plugged daughter, first time in the XL Center,

leery of what was going on, maybe weirded out, a little scared,
but mostly going with it, until they got tired. That's just my XL Center.

If you've been there, you got yours. Maybe The Dead
is playing. Whitney Houston. Taylor Swift. The XL Center

has seen them all, going back to when it was the Hartford
Civic Center, before money renamed it the XL Center,

removed the city's name the way the nod to vets was erased
in the change before that. Walking out of the XL Center

that night, ears ringing, throat sore, I looked ahead
to next time, maybe in Philly, my hometown, or the XL Center

on another tour—the two of them continually side-by-side,
little white dude and Black ex-footballer making the XL Center,

for a few hours, a world in which such a bond
wasn't an anomaly, a world bigger than the XL Center,

where we could all *feel and think and love and dream big*, freed,
bounding from our seats, bouncing at the XL Center,

smiling, singing. The only way to live is without fear of the end,
to sing within the moments we're given, in the XL Center

or elsewhere, to breathe in every good thing and hold
it as long as we can. While every note played in the XL Center

fades back into the nothing it comes from, some echo in your head,
like Clarence's sweet outro while I twirled my little girl at the XL Center

within a sea of swirling lights, my hand over her head, her hand
stretched to mine, everything all right that night at the XL Center.

Clare Rossini

Hartford International University for Religion and Peace

Some of us mull ways to make bucks. Others aspire
to a pistou Provencal
or an antique mirror, its silver flaking off like snow.

Richard Meier had a thing
for light and space. So when it came time to invent a building—
a seminary, say—

he imagined rooms tarnished pink at dawn, corridors crossed
by sunlight, lecterns livid
with dusky flames.

I pace the building's periphery one day in June. White walls
rear up, banks of windows
glaze black in the sun—

perched among broad green lawns,
the seminary seems alien,
abstract as an equation. Yet inside, the seminarians say,

Light seems to come from everywhere.

David Cappella

The Hartford Steam Boiler Building

I

Kaboom! Steam boilers burst!
Industrial hazard! Equipment breakdown!
One explosion every four days!
The age demanded higher pressure, more power—
Twin foundation for The Hartford Steam Boiler Building.

Ah, in 1866, the "blessed assurance" of insurance to the rescue.

In 1932, depression-era money built the HSBB.
A somber Art Deco mixture of cement and steel,
accoutrement of the era, arose on 56 Prospect Street.
The edifice—symmetric, rectangular—
a stolid symbol of no-frills function.

Its offices held brokers and agents
to handle the physical and financial damage
with guarantees against property loss.
The money, lots of money, to be made from an idea:
combine boiler inspections with indemnity.
(That is, for property, not workers!)

The building sits heavy, as though
plopped down from the sky
instead of built up from the site.
An unemotional cube with black eyes.
Stare long enough at the building
an eerie image of Soviet realist style appears.

II

Progress! Growth! Newness!
And a different location to show it.
This is America after all.
The company's tentacles had spread
beyond the city, state, and country.
So: a high rise of twenty-four stories,
dead center in the city's central business district
to overlook the beloved Connecticut River—
a shining badge of financial prowess,
of the hedge against loss (Ah, Capitalism!)

Rectangles, giant windows, reflections!
The geometry of modernism stripped
of ornamentation. It's a SPACE:
optically self-referential, complex
in its simplicity; individual
in its uniformity. The company
occupies the top five floors.

The managing partner notes:
"We're looking forward to building
innovative space that will foster
team-building, mentorship, and collaboration,
and will enhance the hybrid work model
through state-of-the-art technology."
The signature foundation for the new,
          glamorous,
                    state-of-art
Hartford Steam Boiler Building.

Brian Clements

Poems about buildings

are poems about the places where the buildings stand,
what stood there before, what will stand there in ten years,

the nothing that stood on the site of an old farm in Newington in 1898
before Newington Home for Incurables opened with nineteen residents

and withstood a flood of the juvenile poor with tuberculosis,
epilepsy, injuries, some of whom could not stand,

Virginia Thrall Smith standing before the state of Connecticut
and the CT Children's Aid Society to pronounce the need,

what years earlier stood in place of McDonalds on Washington Street
when an architect stood on Hartford Hospital grounds

and imagined how the new building would stand,
imagined children who would pass beneath the cattywampus pavilion,

and into the entryway, trepidatious, to check in with security,
the agony of the child and the agony of the parent there to check the
          child into care,

and walk or wheel down the hall to the elevators
in a building that stands on a foundation that will allow it to double in
          vertical size

for the many children in need but also for the one child who someday
will be taken down from her bed and rolled into rehab

and for the first time in days or weeks or months
stand.

Gian Lombardo

Done with Quiet Moments, No One Dares Leave the Stoops Hungry

Belief bedevils belief. Others had these rooms. That's before. Before lines fell this way and that draped with yesterday's clothes.

Zia Dia knew all the stories. And knew how to put one letter after the other so they could walk on water across the ocean.

Who hangs out a window, calling others home, when the panes are shattered and frames splintered?

They followed other letters. They went where gutturals and fricatives ordered them.

Always the work.

Work.

Ghosts seek someone to sing for them. Harmony, the hardest.

What works best. After rest.

Everyone who comes by, ghost or not, attacks the plate set before them. When does latticed brickwork become a salvation placed alongside desperation?

It does not matter whether they rose before the sun or after. It does not matter if Dia's husband came home on the last trolley from Manchester.

Day is done. Work is done. Belief is the bread in the right hand, and cheese in the other.

Find your way home. The room's swept clean. And no fresh sign hangs from the doorway.

Front Street, 1921

Pegi Deitz Shea

The Ghost of Dunkin' Park—Bob Ferguson, Captain of the Hartford Dark Blues:

Been wonderin' about that night sky aglow upriver
from our Colt baseball grounds. Heard tell of a park
ten times bigger. Hogwash! Nearly 150 years gone
since I joined the Dark Blues. Time to see about the fuss.

Holy mackerel! Tall lamps upon lamps, and no gas fire.
All classes and ages of folks dressed in loony green,
fancy seats for everybody. Little boys—girls, too—
not having to climb trees for a peek at the game.

Music thumps and blares. Where's the bandstand?
A voice booms from—Jeepers!—the clouds.
Here come the players dashing onto the field,
their faces and numbers flashing on a huge board.

What—Negro players as well as White.
Spaniards, Orientals, too. Ain't that curious.
The crowd cheers for them all. Pretty nifty—
6000 people here today just loving the Yard Goats.

Clever name—mighty wee engines shuffling locomotives
and cars on the rails. Trains took us all over—
Chicago, Philadelphia, Boston, and New York.
Reckon real goats are tough enough, ornery as heck.

Hey, these sluggers can slam 'em! Bats still made of ash?
Look at them fellas sprinting and stealing bases!
Fielders had better nab those liners—gloves big as nets,
cushy as pillows, too. These players are mollycoddled.

A new pitcher? Why, there's a whole pen of them.
In my day, one pitcher hurled game after game.
Glad to still see the curve our Cummings invented.
And more tricky pitches—fireballs that move!

Oooeee, I need shade, water, bite to eat. What's this—
winter air inside? … A tavern? I won't stand for it!
Drinkers and gamblers should be chased off the grounds.
Have a care, boys! Especially around the ladies. But …

that roast beef sure smells scrumptious. I don't have a card
to buy me some—I'll just snatch a piece or two, top it off
with a coffee and a dozen of those edible *munchkins*.
An elevator? Rode my first one in New York as a munchkin.

Down two levels, cool as a cave, secret caverns, passages.
I'll be darned—a wide hall for batting balls into nets.
A chamber with newfangled barbells, a ward for doctoring,
rooms for bathing, dressing, even indoor out-housing!

Each player has seven pairs of shoes—some spiked (Smart!),
five gloves, six bats, scads of socks, countless uniforms
(*Los Chivos?*). And machines to wash and dry them all?
What in tarnation? Dirt is a badge of honor!

See here, I like the enclosed field like ours, lamps
for night games, moving pictures, kids petting kid goats,
even everyone dancing and singing about good ole YMCA,
but enough hullabaloo! Wait … a Dark Blues Diner, and

pictures of our team—me, switch-hittin' Bob. Aw, shucks.
Signs saying Dunkin' voted best ballpark time and again,
best attendance with hundreds of thousands of fans
each year …. I'm getting downright misty.

A roar! We won! Whoopee! Fireworks burst above.
Let's celebrate. Hey buddy, got a light for my cigar?
No smoking inside? Well, I should have a care, myself.
I'll snatch an ice cream sundae in a ball cap instead!

Srinivas Mandavilli

The Bone and Joint Institute at Hartford Hospital

I have decided to be happy because it is good for my health. —Voltaire

You marvel at the illusion of the waterwall
    under a stucco ceiling. In this saurian
        atrium, a collage of X-rays conjures up calcific

and osseous densities. You see patients transition
    into motion, their bones welded by orthopedic
        surgeons with titanium rods.

In this circumference of curved corridors, nurses
    pore over recovery from a battle of bodies and pain.
        You pass a balcony of terrazzo and dark wood, brimmed

with light seeping in through sheer patterned glass.
    A skybridge tethers the edifice like a ligament, as it squats
        with its mysteries within textured patterns and glass

formations that twist away. The garbled
    blare of an ambulance makes its way along
        the half-empty street. Looking over, you see a nurse

on her break in the nature garden, the one who held
    your arm that day when your arm needed to be touched
        in a certain way. In the breeze, her coat rises like a cape.

Davyne Verstandig

UCONN Hartford

Out of the remains of marbled old news
of heart-rending stories of birth and death
misfortune and success
power and tragedy
rose a gloried building where students
from 106 countries and nearly 50 states
jostled and streamed through its halls
where racial and religious diversity
were as common as seeing a student drinking
a DD or Starbucks' coffee

As its first students and professors
we experienced a sense of discovery and ownership
in this recreated building
where light shone deep into its corners
courtyards and classrooms
the light of intelligence and understanding

The Structures

Old State House

Main Street

Architectural historians say that the Old State House stands as the most notable structure in the Capital City. Yet today its stature has declined. Its distinguishing feature remains that it faces the Connecticut River, not Main Street. This orientation from a different time in the city's history must confuse contemporary tourists. The confusion continues inside where a hodge-podge of past and present commingles. One can rent the elegant former courtroom where the Amistad case began for a cocktail-party. So many significant moments in American and Connecticut history occurred in this building such as the Hartford Convention of 1815, the 1818 Connecticut Constitution, the Prudence Crandall debate of 1834, and so on. Although frequently altered and renovated and repurposed, this majestic building designed by Charles Bulfinch in 1792 and completed under the oversight of master builder John Leffingwell in 1796, served the state until 1878 and the city until 1915, after that date it had been threatened with demolition several times, but in 1961 the Connecticut Historical Society came to the rescue. Yes, it has been altered many times in its history and even now has a brightly colored but outdated exhibition on Hartford in its lower level. Nonetheless, this historic Neo-Classical style edifice deserves preservation in perpetuity.

Butler-McCook House

Main Street

It has often been stated that geographical mobility is a central aspect of the American character. For example, the French sociologist Jean Baudrillard said that "the American child roams far and wide" and "moving around is [an American's] natural occupation." Not so for the Butler-McCook family who resided at their Main Street domicile for two centuries. Though the family remained in one place, the house itself changed repeatedly for fashion and family. Many renovations and additions to the original structure of 1782 resulted in a conglomeration of styles ranging from twin chimneys typical of the Revolutionary era to an added third floor with a central projecting gable and, last, a one-story doctor's office dating from the early twentieth century. Passed down to generations of Butlers and McCooks, the house reflects the family's ever-changing stylistic tastes, professional vocations, and intellectual curiosities. The unusually large urban setting, achieved after several purchases of surrounding lots, made possible Jacob Weidenmann's garden design of 1865. Weidenmann, who also designed nearby Bushnell Park, created a perfect spot for an outdoor evening concert at this remarkably well-preserved historic house museum, now owned and operated by Connecticut Landmarks.

Center Church

Main Street

This harmonious meeting house, First Church of Christ Congregational, known as Center Church, descends from Reverends Hooker and Stone's original pastorate of 1632 located in Cambridge, Massachusetts. The present building in Hartford replaced an earlier structure (1737) on this site at the corner of the old burying ground. Attributed to Daniel Wadsworth and built by John Leffingwell in 1807, the church embodies classical federal style elements including an Ionic portico with pediment and stepped opulent tall spire. The interior repeats classical Ionic design motifs with more decorative additions in 1852 and six prismatic Tiffany windows installed between 1894-1903. The overall effect adds up to an inspiring house of worship. The sanctuary's current organ built by Austin Organs, Inc. of Hartford dates from 1954. Frederick Douglass spoke outside the church in 1843. As he said, we "determined to hold our meetings under the open sky, which we did in a little court under the eaves of the sanctuary … " A plaque memorializes this occasion. Today the church continues to hold weekly services and is a center for the arts and the community as well as a thriving spiritual center.

Wadsworth Atheneum

Main Street

The Connecticut artist Sol Le Witt, Hartford born, frequently visited the Atheneum (one of his wall paintings greets all visitors to the museum) and once reportedly remarked that although he enjoyed the Atheneum all his life, he always got lost inside. Like many grand art museums, the five buildings of the Hartford institution have a labyrinthine quality to them and if overall they form a maze, the initial building designed by Ithiel Town and Alexander Jackson Davis has the appearance of a castle. The Avery Memorial (1934) follows the program of the International Style and omits ornament. There have been attempts to unify the styles and interiors of the buildings, most recently in 1991 and then again in 2015, the latter partly the work of Tyler Smith, a champion of Hartford history and preservation. Of course, the art museum is not only the structure itself, but the artwork displayed therein and with a collection that has grown from Daniel Wadsworth's Hudson River School paintings to fifty-thousand objects from across the globe and time periods and forms. As Sally Van Doren puts it in her poem, "Circles and majestic / semi-circles soften the angles / of the walls peopled with old masters / in gilded frames." If the Wadsworth Atheneum remains a maze—like so many other large urban art institutions, this one is a good one to step inside and get lost in for an afternoon. It is true too that others see this group of five buildings in a very different light. Anne Crofoot Kuckro noted in *Hartford Architecture* (1978): "The Wadsworth Atheneum is the most complex and well-integrated cluster of buildings in Downtown. The five buildings in this group were built over a period of 126 years, and their designs are each individual and distinctive, but work together to create a whole better than the sum of its parts."

Asylum Hill Congregational Church

Asylum Avenue

Built as the Civil War came to an end, this large church in the Gothic style differs from most others serving this denomination. Here instead of plain and simple, the congregant worships in an extremely rich and ornamental interior. Its Irish-born architect Patrick Keely designed hundreds of Catholic churches throughout New York and New England. Today the website pictures two sacraments—baptism and communion—as if to set the record straight. It is a Congregational church and not a Catholic or Episcopal one, despite the high style of dark wood and stained-glass. When Rev. Joseph Twichell retired after forty-six years at Asylum Hill, his colleague and friend Reverend Edwin Pond Parker of the more traditional in appearance South Congregational Church also retired though at an even fifty years of service to his congregation. The *Brooklyn Eagle* noted in 1911 regarding both men: "The clergyman who keeps his hold on a particular Congregational church for fifty years or forty-six years, must be a diplomat as well as a scholar and a preacher, for at any time, without consulting any central authority, a Congregational body is free to make a change. Dr. Twitchell," the *Eagle* article continued, "leaves no factions in his church." And today senior minister Erica Thompson tries to "ignite the flame in others so that we might all go out into the world illuminating the way of hope … " Sheathed in brownstone from Portland, Connecticut, Asylum Hill Congregational Church has looked out to its neighborhood, state, and world for more than one-hundred and fifty years.

Colt Armory

Van Dyke and Huyshope Avenues

The primary architectural focus of the Colt complex of buildings is the East Armory, which today faces Interstate 91. At the height of the company's success this structure was surrounded by a host of buildings that provided everything from power, transportation, housing, provisions and religion to the skilled workforce employed at the Armory. A fire in 1864 two years after Samuel Colt's death, prompted his beloved wife, Elizabeth, to spearhead reconstruction in 1867. The East Armory is similar in design to the original building designed by Hartford architect Octavius Jordan. Today the most prominent feature of this excellent example of mid-nineteenth century architecture is the blue onion dome, perched on a circle of white columns and topped by a reproduction of the original rampant colt on a gold sphere. It caps the three and one-half story brick and brownstone building with a noticeable vertical thrust marked by rows of large rectangular windows. A central projecting gable flanked by strong cross gables provided natural light to 500 by 60-foot rooms on each level with rows of 60 cast iron columns originally supporting shafting for steam engines. While the monumentality of the East Armory is a sight to behold, its history belies a story which perpetuates firearms violence in our country still pervasive today. Colt Armory production hummed for many years. Even before the Armory's rebuilding, Colt manufactured over 136,000 guns at the height of the Civil War in 1863. At least with the Thomas Hooker Taproom now on site, beer now flows out instead of bullets. Recall that for the poet Wallace Stevens the nearby Church of the Good Shepherd would be better named St. Armorer's Church: "once an immense success." Once, too, the Colt company provided housing for its employees. The Potsdam Village of 1858, for example, meant to attract and retain skilled German workers. We may deplore the paternalism of the mid-nineteenth century and the many covenants of mid-twentieth century construction of Kaiser Community Homes and Levitt & Sons, but our builders complain a 10,000 square foot house is the only possibility for profit. Everyone has a cellphone in hand, but fewer are those with a roof over their head. Employers need employees, but employees can't afford the price of a place to live. These facts result from policy, policy and politics. "We have reached a point ... where the single-family home is outdated," Frances Anderton writes in her recent study of multifamily housing. She continues, "it gobbles up land and resources; if is financially out of reach for most young—and older—people ... " Maybe housing should supersede the call for a National Park.

Harriet Beecher Stowe House

Forest Street

In December of 1872, Harriet Beecher Stowe wrote her children regarding the Forest Street house, "Everybody says it is a valuable property & rising in value & it is a lovely beautiful house & the terms are quite within my means." Before purchasing this simple Gothic cottage, the Stowes resided in an elaborate home that proved too expensive for them. Stowe's words to her children reveal a mix of an ideal and the real. For an author who wrote extensively about the importance of a well-appointed home, the Forest Street abode exhibits a simplified Gothic exterior, and this simplicity repeats in the interior. Harriet Beecher Stowe earned most of the family's income and she described this house as both "beautiful" and a sound investment. In the prior decade throughout her *Atlantic Monthly* series (later published in book form) she emphasized that "a true home should be called the noblest work of art." Yet, whereas Stowe claimed that "homes are the work of art peculiar to the genius of women," her Hartford grandniece Charlotte Perkins Gilman in her poem "To the Young Wife" described a woman's domestic life as a "paltry queenship in the narrow place." Another grandniece, Katherine Seymour Day, acknowledged Stowe's advocacy of women's prominent role in the home and her great-aunt's role in the abolition of slavery with her dedication to the restoration of the home and the beginning of the Stowe-Day Foundation. Today's repurposed house tour not only includes Stowe's position on domesticity and her abolitionism, but also asks visitors to reflect on their relevance to today's social issues.

Windsor Avenue Congregational Church / Faith Congregational Church

Main Street

Katie Day, a scholar of American religious history, has written that "communities of faith contribute to the social well-being of individuals, neighborhoods and cities in ways that should be identified and publicly appreciated ... " A house of faith offers more than services and study of texts. Such community institutions offer a place to gather and meet and share the company and joy of being with others even in—or especially in—times of struggle and adversity. Windsor Avenue, now known as Main Street, features several elegant post-bellum church edifices in addition to the Congregational Church, including Saint Thomas Episcopal Church (Union Baptist), 1871, and Metropolitan African Methodist Episcopal, 1874. The Windsor Avenue Congregation Church, 1871, included among its earliest congregants Harriet Beecher Stowe who attended services, especially to hear her son Charles E. Stowe preach. Its architectural design by Samuel J. F. Taylor of Boston abides by the principles of the High Victorian reform movement that promoted accurate medieval Gothic form to instill spiritual fervor—which seems too high style for a Congregational meeting house. This spiritual Gothic mode became often associated in America with mid-nineteenth-century Episcopal buildings such as John Notman's 1848-51 St. Marks Church of Philadelphia. Taylor, on the other hand, wrote, "I have studied to give great force to the design with simple details." Simple or elaborate, in 1953 Hartford's oldest African American church relocated here, and undertook devoted stewardship of the building. As Proverbs (24:3-4) has it: "By wisdom a house is built, and by understanding it is established; by knowledge the rooms are filled with precious and pleasant riches." The richest of all may be the community of saints therein. The current congregation (1953) traces its origin back to the Talcott Street Congregational Church (1826), where in 1829 Rev. James Pennington, an escaped slave who became the first Black recipient of an honorary doctorate from the University of Heidelberg, opened Hartford's first school for African-American children.

Mark Twain House

Farmington Avenue

In May of 1929 the *Hartford Courant* noted that "it was about ten years ago that an artist, Nunzio Vayana ... conceived the purchase and preservation of the home." Wait a minute. Nunzio who? What about Katherine Seymour Day? Day, also an artist, contributed the money; Vayana, the organization. She, a Nativist, is remembered; Vayana, an immigrant, is not. Money talks. Don't tourists at Hartford's number one tourist site wonder how much those interiors by Louis Comfort Tiffany's firm Associated Artists would cost in today's dollars? Vayana made a life-size bust of Mark Twain that wrapped in American flag bunting stood in front of the Twain house in 1920. It was stolen and never returned, as was any recollection of this Italian immigrant. You won't find him on the tour or the website. And when Robert Stern designed the 32,700-square-foot Museum Center in 2003 for the Edward Tuckerman Potter 11,500-square-foot 1873 house, land had to be appropriated, annexed from the neighboring Hartford Public High School. The Museum building received LEED Certification from the United States Green Building Council, the first museum structure to do so. The house itself has seven bathrooms among its twenty-five rooms. Its red and black exterior recalls the skin of a salamander. One newspaper in 1929 noted that "Years ago no one in Hartford gave the proposed destruction of Mark Twain's home a thought, with the exception of a big-hearted and underappreciated artist by the name of Nunzio Vayana."

Lucy Barbour House

Beacon Street

Down this street of Halloween houses rests one that once housed a school for girls. This Italianate structure has none of the horror of collegiate Gothic. Once voices must have echoed in Lucy Barbour's School for Girls. Now, the house has been broken into several rental units. Originally located in a house farther south on Beacon, the school had to move north to accommodate a quickly increasing number of students. At its height, it had five teachers and thirty-eight pupils, including Edna Cooke, daughter of Connecticut's governor at the time. Students studied French, German, and Latin; math, history, English literature, and science. According to an article published on August 14, 1897 in the *Hartford Courant*: "The school aims to inspire thoroughness in its members, and they have certainly done much faithful work, no less satisfactory to their teachers than to themselves." Architecture can be defined as shelter with ornament. That definition fits this building, a box with projecting porch, ascending arch, and hipped roof. Its simple sculptural integrity appeals to a passerby's eye any day of the year.

Charter Oak Cultural Center

Charter Oak Avenue

At the moment there are more than a half-dozen former religious buildings for sale in Hartford from Catholic to Jewish to Seventh Day Adventist and from structures of historic significance to a converted storefront chapel. One of these can be purchased for a mere single-dollar, but the purchaser must move it elsewhere. Congregation Beth Israel of Harford moved from its 1876 home to the suburb of West Hartford in 1936. Designed by Hartford architect George Keller, the original structure was the first building in the state built as a synagogue. After the congregation moved, the Calvary Baptist Church used it until they, too, abandoned the building in the 1970s. The city planned to demolish it, but a small group of leaders in the local Jewish community came to the rescue and planned to revive the edifice as a neighborhood center, now a multicultural arts center. Keller was not the first choice for the temple's design, but when the cost of the original architect's design exceeded the budget, the selection committee purchased a Keller proposal. The synagogue, in the Romanesque style, has domed twin towers and round-arched windows on its façade. Constructed of brownstone, red brick, and limestone, these exterior materials, as the architectural historian David Ransom wrote, "express the Victorian love of polychromy." Stenciling of the interior echoes the attention to color seen on the exterior. Expanded in 1899 and restored in the late 1970s, today the Charter Oak Cultural Center is, as their mission statement puts it, "a vibrant place of community whose mission is explicitly to do the work of social justice through the arts."

Cheney Building

Main Street

Steve Straight told us: "It is a gorgeous place for a brewery." Fred Astaire used to sing: "How I love a glass of beer. Beer goes very good with beer." But to continue with what Steve Straight told us: "When I went in and mentioned to the manager what I was doing, he gave me a terrific tour of the whole building, even the cellar." Ah, yes—the building. Local preservationist David Ransom claimed that "architecture critics would undoubtedly vote the Cheney Block, designed by America's greatest 19th-century architect, the finest building in Hartford." Anne Crofoot Kuckro of the Hartford Architecture Conservancy concurred though a little less emphatically. In the late 1970s she called the Cheney Building "a powerful statement, reflecting the vigor and vitality of the Hartford business community and establishing Richardson Romanesque as the most popular style in Hartford" during the final quarter of the nineteenth century. Three design elements define this monumental structure: its semi-circular arches (hence, the Romanesque), its use of brownstone with limestone accents, and its carefully orchestrated fenestration. The Cheney Building has always been a mixed-use building of retail and office space and sometimes apartments, too. The land once was home to a Baptist Church. Now the rehabilitated Cheney Building has not only a brewery, but a comedy club aptly named the Brew HaHa. Well, at least, it had until March 31, 2024, when the brewery closed due to a four-month closure after a sprinkler pipe burst and flooded the building. Fear not, for when the business opened there were only two brew pubs in Connecticut and today there are more than 130 of them. Yes, "beer goes very good with beer."

Saint Patrick's and Saint Anthony's Church

Church Street

This Gothic Revival brownstone church replaced an earlier structure that had burned to the ground. The prolific religious architect Patrick Keely who designed Asylum Hill Congregational (1865) and the original Saint Joseph Cathedral (1892) prepared the plans for Saint Patrick's and Saint Anthony's (1876). Originally named for the former saint, it took on the combined name in 1958 during an ecclesiastical consolidation. The church traces its origin to 1829, the oldest Catholic parish in Connecticut. At its beginning and through its first decades it served Irish immigrants whereas Saint Anthony's ministered to Italian immigrants beginning in the 1890s. In 1990, Franciscan Friars took charge of the parish and created a vibrant urban ministry. As Father Tim Shreenan, pastor of the parish, wrote: "I often like to say that the Eucharist, the summit and source of our lives as Catholic Christians, affords us the opportunity and challenge to be bread for the world."

Connecticut State Capitol

Capitol Avenue

The gold dome of the State Capitol glistens in the sun and proclaims, as architectural historian Christopher Wigren has written, "Connecticut's wealth and taste, a monument to its proud past, and an ornament for the city of Hartford." Historic motifs such as the Charter Oak tree, the State Seal, and a star design compass that symbolizes unity appear repeatedly throughout the building in carvings, carpets, glass, and stone. In 1876 Hartford became the sole capital, ending a long history of sharing the honor, since 1701, with New Haven. Two years later, the wonderful new Capitol opened. Its original plan by Richard Michell Upjohn underwent controversial alteration led by Hartford entrepreneur James G. Batterson (whose East Canaan quarry supplied the marble). The notable gold dome, for example, replaced Upjohn's conventional clock tower. The building's beautiful interior features extensive chromatic stenciling, grand staircases, expansive public space for ease of circulation with many significant artifacts and relics adorning those spaces. In sum, the overall impression created by the architecture both on the exterior and interior fosters a strong sense of civic pride. The house and senate chambers embody the spirit of democratic government which carries through to the 1988 Legislative Office Building, meeting the working needs of legislators and their staffs. Known as the LOB, this companion building designed by Russell Gibson von Dohlen of Farmington, compliments and repeats the iconography of the Capitol and—along with the adjoining State Armory (1909) and the nearby State Library and Supreme Court (1910)—completes the assemblage of state governmental buildings along Capitol Avenue—all of which inspire civic participation.

Soldiers and Sailors Memorial Arch

Ford Street

Isn't it strange that an architect, George Keller, so well-known for funerary memorials should have had such a horror of cemeteries that his and his wife's, Mary, ashes are interred in a monument beside Bushnell Park dedicated to Hartford soldiers and sailors of the Civil War? This first triumphal arch in America mixes several styles—including Gothic and Romanesque – to create a unified tribute. Keller had been commissioned for notable monuments in other locations and did not participate in a competition for Hartford's. When submissions exceeded the project budget, Keller responded with one of his own that met budgetary limits. Beginning from his friend Rev. Francis Goodwin's idea of a bridge and arch, Keller moved the proposed arch to solid ground and utilized brownstone and terra cotta in cost saving measures. One side of the frieze shows soldiers at war and the other, at peace. Keller replaced one of six large statues, a merchant, with a Black man breaking his chains of bondage with one hand and with a school slate in the other hand. Near this statue a plaque commemorates the 128 African Americans from Hartford who served in the Union Army. The Arch must have looked much more spectacular and dramatic prior to 1938, when the Park River was re-located underground. The moving water of the small river must have added a picturesque quality to memorial. In 1931 Keller received his final commission: the base for the nearby Lafayette memorial on Capitol Avenue.

Union Station

Union Place

In 1889, the newly constructed Union Station symbolized the commercial and industrial success of Hartford in the late nineteenth century. Replacing an earlier structure, the new station elevated previous ground-level tracks, which posed a danger to street level traffic, an idea suggested by Hartford architect George Keller. The train station building, constructed of New England brownstone, embodies the massive, but simple forms of the Richardson Romanesque style conceived and designed by the Boston firm of Shepley, Rutan & Coolidge, successors to the architectural practice led by Henry Hobson Richardson. Like many of Hartford's notable historic buildings, Union Station underwent several transformations over the years. A large, destructive fire in 1914 necessitated an almost total rebuild and added second and third floors. As Hartford witnessed a decline in commerce, Union Station fell into disrepair. By 1954 one visitor to the city described the structure as a "useless monstrosity." It was not until 1965, under new ownership, that the station underwent a major renovation, involving removal of the original benches in the Great Room, creating a large open center space. Again, new ownership in 1985 resulted in another major restoration expanding the building's function and making it a multi-use transportation center with the addition of bus service and leasing of offices on the upper floors. Decades long construction of interstate highways bordering Hartford, the popularity of malls, preference for remote work, and the introduction of sophisticated technology all have combined to supplant Union Station as the region's center of transport. Nonetheless, the station remains a travel hub for those seeking the convenience of letting someone else do the driving.

The Linden

Main Street

One Hartford newspaper reported in 1892 that "the Linden is a model apartment house." The owners of the famed department store Brown, Thompson, & Company developed this five-story up-to-date residential structure with echoes of the Cheney Building. The apartment building's Romanesque design features a rhythmical arrangement of windows accentuated by the placement of square turrets above the cornice. Alternating red and black bricks add depth and texture to its rhythm. Originally, The Linden contained fifty-nine apartments, as the newspaper put it: units "are light and airy and from some the view is delightful." After its 1980s renovation, there are now fifty-one units that have exposed brick walls, sleeping lofts, and all the modern conveniences. One unit even comes with a rooftop turret room. Though the dwellings are bright, the building feels dark and heavy, weighty as a fortress. One walks by this substantial edifice, pauses, and wonders who lives here? Maybe that's something to ponder while dining in the historic building's ground-floor restaurant.

Saint Francis Hospital

Woodland Street

Our guess is that most residents think of 1000 Asylum Avenue when they think of Saint Francis Hospital, but from 1941 to 1974 that building in fact belonged to the National Fire Insurance Company. The Dillion Memorial of 1938 around the corner on Woodland Street might be a better choice for the architectural heart of this complex, today the largest Catholic hospital in New England. Modern buildings like the 2008 ten story John T. O'Connell Tower diminish the older, smaller Georgian Revival building with Madonna and Child at its entrance. Local architect Michael J. Crosbie has noted that Louis A. Walsh, a child of Irish immigrants who designed the Dillion Memorial and many other Catholic institutional buildings in Connecticut, "was a good, ordinary architect who designed a lot of good, ordinary buildings." Some patients prefer Saint Francis to other area hospitals because of its affiliation – its ordinary goodness, if you will. In 1990 Saint Francis formed a link with Mount Sinai Hospital, the first collaboration in the United States between a Catholic hospital and a Jewish hospital. A former president and chief executive officer, David D'Eramo, said, "We pride ourselves on being a comprehensive teaching hospital with a social conscience and a strong sense of mission." The subsequent president, Thomas Burke, has reiterated this purpose: "We continue to honor Core Values: Reverence, Commitment to those who are poor, Safety, Justice, Stewardship, and Integrity. Regardless of the growth we've seen between the hospital that was founded in 1897 and the Saint Francis of today, that Mission and those Core Values remain top of mind." On the night of August 1, 1955, Peter Hanchak and his mother Holly Stevens visited the Saint Francis room of their grandfather/father, Wallace Stevens. The poet-businessman suffering from cancer had regained consciousness. As Peter Brazeau wrote in *Parts of a World: Wallace Stevens Remembered*, "they all wished each other goodnight. At eight-thirty the next morning, Wallace Stevens died."

Keney Memorial Clock Tower

Main Street

The name Keney, according to an obituary for Henry (1806-1894), "has been for years the common property of Hartford, part of the business reputation of which the city is so reasonably proud." The Keney brothers, Harry and Walter (1809-1889), owned a successful wholesale grocery business and participated in other commercial ventures. Leaving no heirs, the brothers donated most of the land for the park that bears their name and at the site of their home, they directed the trustees of their estate to erect a "suitable and proper memorial ... to perpetuate the memory of the firm of H. & W. Keney." Interestingly, the dedication plaque inside the tower memorializes their mother. Thirty feet square and 130 feet tall, the free-standing tower, designed by Charles C. Haight in the Gothic Revival style and constructed with Longmeadow, Massachusetts sandstone, houses a Seth Thomas clock from Thomaston, Connecticut. In the early 1990s a diligent restoration used a toothbrush and corncobs to clean surfaces. Clock hands on all four faces had gold leaf reapplied. The fence surrounding the one and one-half acre park received a fresh coat of paint and broken windows were replaced. In 2019, University of Connecticut engineering students repaired the clock and its bells. The earlier renovation had disconnected the weights that operated the chimes and installed a computerized sound system that played songs, hymns, and Christmas carols as well as marked time. The engineering students restored the original bells. Parts for the historic clock had to be re-invented and made from currently available materials to match nineteenth-century functions. Now the chimes sound once again, and the students got an A. Even the bird of prey gargoyles atop the four corners of the cornice are, for now, happy.

Perfect Sixes

Mortson Street, Park Terrace, and Putnam Heights

Journalist and state representative Christine Palm once said that "Hartford is justifiably proud of its legacy of the perfect six," a sort of double triple decker found throughout the city but predominantly located in Frog Hollow. Yet, these sturdy structures from nearly a century and a quarter ago have confronted a continuous cycle of boom and bust or, rather, repair and despair. Originally, they housed an emerging middle-class of skilled workers and their families. For example, in Frog Hollow innovative industries such as Hart & Hegeman, Pope Manufacturing, and Pratt & Whitney were within walking distance. As companies closed or relocated, the perfect sixes became over-crowded and then fell into a state of imperfection. In the latter part of the twentieth-century community non-profits rehabilitated and restored some of these properties. On occasion, completing the refurbishing several times. These three-story brick buildings with exterior exposure on four sides and bow or bay windows flanking an entry porch usually have a sheet metal cornice or a brick gable that adds a picturesque quality to the façade. One present day resident of the block long Park Terrace remodeling says, "I love my view of the park and I spend a lot of time on my balcony" and another says about her unit, "It makes you feel better about yourself and makes you want to work, to keep it up. This is my home."

Connecticut State Library and Supreme Court

Capitol Avenue

The Connecticut State Library and Supreme Court Building is perhaps the most imposing structure in Hartford. Today, it is one of the few architectural gems in the city that still serves the purpose for which it was originally designed in 1906 and constructed between 1908-1910. This stately building, the joint work of architects Donn Barber and Edward T. Hapgood in the Beaux-Arts classical style, has always housed Connecticut's highest court, voluminous law and history libraries, vast archival collections, portraits of the state's governors, and, among many historically significant documents, the Fundamental Orders of 1639, which represents an early codification of a bicameral, democratic form of government and is the embodiment of Connecticut's moniker, "The Constitution State." Conceived as the final addition to a trio of government buildings sited on a prominent rise above the city and bordering on the Frog Hollow neighborhood, the Connecticut State Library and Supreme Court Building is a monument to "Knowledge," "History" and "Justice." These representations inscribed in the cornice of the large portico, designate the building's three functions, with the court occupying the right wing, the library in the left wing and the paintings and artifacts in the center wing. Along with the State Capitol (1878) and the Armory (1909) the library and court intentionally formed a government center framed by the City Beautiful movement of the early twentieth century. Aligned closely with the Beaux Arts style, the two intertwined paradigms symbolized classical notions of civic pride, participation and patriotism. The exterior façade with a broad flight of entrance steps leads to a full entablature sporting large Doric columns and allegorical roof-line statuary by Francois Tonette. On the interior, coffered and gilded ceilings impel the visitor to appreciate the plethora of governmental, historical, and judicial material culture that this wonderful building preserves, right down to the artfully executed murals by Albert Herter in the Supreme Court which depict the signing of the Fundamental Orders and an allegorical representation of Education.

G. Fox

Main Street

Seventy years ago, the G. Fox department store advertised itself as "the center of Connecticut living since 1847." In March of 1955 a Barbecue Chef, a large toaster-oven-like contraption, could cook a twenty-pound roast and make anyone "a super chef." Yours on sale for $34.99. A year later and a faille coachman dress "spiced with ivy league striped rayon taffeta lining" provided just the right look "for college or career." As of 2002, after a seventy-million-dollar renovation, the Cass Gilbert neo-classical revival style building of 1918 became the home of Capital Community College, offering 300,000 square feet of classrooms, gathering spaces, laboratories, and academic administration offices. Once the largest privately owned department store in the county, G. Fox & Co. served as a center of community until its closing in 1993. Crowds once enjoyed elaborate Christmas displays and live performances in the vast ground floor atrium, a tour-de-force of Art Deco style resulting from a 1935 refurbishing that also added exterior stainless-steel bands for a streamlined marquee. The cream-colored brick building has eight bays with paired windows, topped with one-story Corinthian columns and pilasters. The current educational function for the building can be viewed as an important contribution to on-going efforts to revitalize downtown Hartford. As Capital Community puts it: the college works to instill "life-changing knowledge in a community of learners from multi-cultural backgrounds in a vital urban setting where business, culture, and government converge."

Travelers Tower

Tower Square / Atheneum Square

In May 1918, when the Travelers Tower neared completion, a daring *Hartford Courant* photographer ascended the structure and noted that when one "gets there and borrows his breath back," one "gets a sweeping panoramic view of Hartford and surrounding towns." Indeed, at the time of its opening in 1919, the tower, rising 527 feet, stood as the tallest skyscraper in New England and remained so until 1964 and in Connecticut until 1984. In addition to offering an outstanding picture of the metro-region, the tower epitomized the rise of the city as the "Insurance Capital" of the nation. And, unlike many other insurance firms that have relocated outside the downtown area, Travelers remains steadfast in maintaining its home office there. Designed by Donn Barber and Edward T. Hapgood, the tower was the final product of a three-stage project involving development of two separate conjoined and identical, five-story office buildings, the first one finished in 1906 and the second, which forms the base of the tower, opened in 1913. In fact, the company's successful growth warranted more office space, a need fulfilled by the tower. Although constructed at different times, the Travelers presents as unified in style due to the ongoing design work of Barber and his use of Neoclassical Renaissance elements, including strong cornices marking each level and repeating rows of fenestration changing in size and configuration. The tower, supported near its top by Ionic columns, has a domed lantern and metal finial. Granite, mined from quarries owned by Travelers founder, James Goodwin Batterson, comprises the entire structure. In the early twentieth century, the mail chute system, large switchboard, bank of six elevators, and fire suppression apparatus that could pump water to all 34 floors, were considered very modern for their time. Over the years, Travelers Tower has hosted thousands of visitors enjoying the panoramic views, alerted many pilots to its height, and even in 1924, served as a fire protection lookout station. A 1963 renovation moved the main entrance from Main Street to Atheneum Square, which at some point was adorned with the famous red umbrella sculpture. Finally, a 2013 massive, multi-million-dollar renovation restored the exterior, returning the Travelers to one of the most recognizable landmarks of the Harford skyline.

The Hartford

Asylum Avenue

The Hartford's move out of downtown and up to Asylum Hill made front page news in 1921. The new headquarters, the *Courant* proclaimed, would be "one of the showpieces of the city." The construction spared "no expense" and used only "the finest materials." Indeed, "a visitor to Hartford [...] might believe that Connecticut has two state capitals" since the two-story portico and central dome created a stately and monumental Classical Revival edifice, the style most often associated with capitol buildings (unlike Connecticut's unique High Victorian Gothic one). The land had been purchased from the American School for the Deaf by one of the oldest insurance companies in the world, founded in 1810. The executive offices were on the first floor. Wallace Stevens's office was to the right of the entrance way. Now other buildings surround the 1921 headquarters. It may be to some who drive by on Asylum Avenue that the 22-story office tower built almost fifty years later dwarfs the earlier structure, casts a shadow upon it. Maybe not. This tower of bronze metal panels and bronze glazing recalls Ludwig Mies van der Rohe's 1958 Seagram Building on Park Avenue in New York City. Today, The Hartford has more than 18,000 employees, not all of them work in the city of Hartford but the company has closed suburban locations in Simsbury and Windsor and centralized more activities at its city corporate campus. It has annexed other nearby buildings such as Benjamin Wistar Morris's 1926 Connecticut Mutual Life and Carl J. Malmfeldt's 1936 Caledonian-American Insurance. The three early twentieth-century buildings each have an impressive portico entrance and use classical architectural vocabulary. Together these buildings along with meticulous landscaping (including the start of the Wallace Stevens Walk) make an attractive corporate campus. Atop the tower, a stag (the corporate icon) looks out across the city and far beyond. The stag makes another appearance at Dunkin' Park in the form of a 1,800-pound statue mounted on the baseball stadium's roof over the Hartford Terrace section of far right-field and from just the right spot you can see this stag looking directly at the one atop the tower off in the distance, a visual effect worthy of Borromini.

Bulkeley High School

Wethersfield Avenue

Several well-known Hartford institutions have had buildings in more than one location, an old and a new building. Hartford Steam Boiler, for example, built an Art Deco headquarters in 1932 and fifty years later moved into a much larger high-rise building. Bulkeley High School's original building opened in 1924 and in 1978 a massive new school opened near the old Collegiate Gothic style school, which then became an elementary school. But Bulkeley's story has three parts, and its conclusion cannot yet be told. In 2019 renovations began while students and staff dispersed to other buildings, essentially separated into different campuses. Bulkeley students felt deprived of a true high school experience. While the late 70s building had decayed and sorely needed reconstruction, students regretted fewer extracurricular activities, loss of an auditorium, a cafeteria, and a biology lab. Meanwhile, construction fell far behind schedule and far, far over budget. As of this writing, the completion date is not in sight. The school's name honors Morgan G. Bulkeley (1837-1922), businessman, politician, and first president of the National Baseball League. We hope the renovation succeeds—hits a homerun, draws students back to school, and ends chronic absenteeism in the district.

Wallace Stevens House

Westerly Terrace

Reverend Pendleton used to have a pig roast in the backyard every summer, but when the Episcopal Church of Connecticut put the former Stevens house and other Hartford properties up for sale to raise cash in a secular time, a small consortium of interested poetry enthusiasts (including the poet's grandson) attempted to purchase the residence on the western edge of the city with the intent of creating a museum. Why not? But, as real estate transactions often do, this deal fell apart at the last minute. One can observe looking at 118 Westerly Terrace that it is not a modest Cape Cod, but neither is it a McMansion. Stevens's domicile reminds us that once upon a time in America, the income gap between executive and average employee was nothing like the disparate abyss that it is today. In one letter from December 1932 Stevens wrote: "We bought a house some time ago out on Westerly Terrace, which is a twig running off from Terry Road, which, you may remember, is a branch running off the main stem of Asylum Avenue. Without launching into any description of the house (which, I suppose, is very much like other houses), it is enough to say that we are delighted with it, although a little short of furniture." Three years later, quite satisfied, he informed the same correspondent: "I never really lived until I had a home, and my own room, say, with a package of books from Paris or London."

Emanuel Synagogue

Woodland Street

Historians often describe American Jewish history in three phases: mid-nineteenth-century German-speaking Jewish immigration followed by late-nineteenth and early twentieth-century Eastern European and Russian Jewish immigration, and, last, the move from urban to suburban after World War II. Emanuel Synagogue aptly represents this progression. In 1927 the congregation moved from a former Methodist Episcopal church to a newly constructed synagogue near Keney Park, in the heart of the Hartford Jewish community. The park served as a communal gathering place for all area synagogues following Saturday services. In 1967 the congregation moved to the suburb of West Hartford after most its members had relocated there. The architects of the commodious 1927 building—it could accommodate 1,000—Ebbets & Frid also designed the West Hartford Town Hall and Library as well as many of the largest private homes in Hartford and West Hartford. The religious vibrancy continues in this gracious well-maintained house of worship as it has gone from cantor to gospel choir, now home to the Faith Seventh Day Adventist Church.

Bushnell Performing Arts Center

Capitol Avenue

In his "Connecticut Tercentenary Ode" recited at the Bushnell or Friday October 11, 1935, Wesleyan English Professor and future Connecticut governor Wilbert Snow claimed, "Connecticut was Jordan and the clear / Streams flowing to it marked the Promised Land." But Snow concluded near the end of his ode, "the promise has not been entirely fulfilled: [...] tell what tears / And laughter rounded out three hundred years / Of new world story whose page we scan /The enduring grief and dignity of man." On the same occasion Yale President James Angell in his keynote address found the source of those tears, that grief to be immigrants who pushed the state far from its Puritan roots. He noted, "There have been very large invasions of foreign stock, to whom the traditional ideals of the Puritan are wholly alien ... " And yet this 1930 building with its Georgian Revival exterior, its Art Deco interior, its architectural echoes of the Old State House, and its 2002 addition of the nine-hundred and six seat Belding Theater to compliment the two-thousand and eight-hundred seat Mortensen Hall, has always been grand enough to host performances by Judy Garland and Luciano Pavarotti and local enough for a mouse to grow into the Sugar Plum Fairy. Much of this graciousness may result from the fine original work Corbett, Harrison, Helme and MacMurry, the same architectural firm that designed New York City's Rockefeller Center.

Hartford Public Library

Main Street

Sometimes the city of Hartford just can't get a break. The library with an extraordinary and long 230-year history has faced too much adversity in recent years. In its past the institution progressed and grew, but less so of late. By the mid-1950s, Schutz & Goodwin of Hartford designed an interesting asymmetrical new home above the Whitehead Highway. The fenestration runs horizontal and vertical creating a Mondrian-like modernist rhythm. By the early 2000s, the building required expansion and renovation. The 2007 result, gracious and imaginative in many ways, suffered contractors' errors, especially in its new flooring. Then slightly more than a decade later, water damage forced a lengthy closure. Despite the setbacks, the 94,448-square-foot 1957 building increased by another 145,000 square feet in 2007, and the expansion included an attractive large lecture space, the Contemporary Culture Room, a new home for the Hartford History Collection, and a neat Skywalk Art Gallery. The library has been a blessing for immigrants to Connecticut and UCONN Hartford students. A highlight of recent years has been the installation of two Romare Bearden murals relocated from the XL Center. Commissioned by the city in 1980, the large works necessitated the removal of a bank of windows to get them into the building during October 2014. The library began long ago under the guidance of Connecticut luminaries such as Daniel Wadsworth and Timothy Dwight, and now, as the library's own words state, "Hartford Public Library's history continues to be distinguished by its service to the community and by the community's enduring commitment to it."

Constitution Plaza

At the time it seemed like a good idea, though one which the citizens of Hartford, as during other redevelopment schemes that followed, had little say in. The demolition of over two hundred buildings in 1959 destroyed a vibrant multi-ethnic neighborhood. Today this area is devoid of activity and energy except for the weekend of Hartford Tastes, an annual food festival. As of this writing, one whole building is vacant. While notable Hartford companies such as Travelers, Aetna, and the Hartford, carry on in their long-standing locations, Hartford Steam Boiler and Phoenix Mutual have been sold. One of the Plaza's original landmarks, Broadcast House, was demolished after its occupant, WFSB, moved to a suburban location in Rocky Hill. Despite ownership changes, remodeling, and repurposing, Constitution Plaza has struggled to find an identity. Nonetheless, as architectural historian Christopher Wigren has said, "landscape elements gave Constitution Plaza a greater degree of coordination than many similar projects." Its design elements including a continuous above ground podium linked by walkways and plantings and punctuated by a cloak tower and fountain designed by Masao Kimoshita, provide a coherent and appealing setting for the modernist structures overseen by coordinating architect Charles DuBose of Hartford. The scale of the project, praised by civic and corporate leaders at the time of its construction, doomed it because its ambitions were too large for the site and for such a small city. Perhaps in Atlanta or Boston it might have meant more success and longevity? In the post-pandemic world with workplaces transformed, there is little hope that the approximately 1,800 underground parking spaces will ever reach capacity, nor will the Plaza contribute to a Hartford revival.

Cathedral of Saint Joseph

Farmington Avenue

Regarding her poem, Sharon L. Charde notes that "on December 31, 1956, Saint Joseph Cathedral, a beautiful Gothic-style brownstone, caught fire and was destroyed, rebuilt in 1962 as a cold modern concrete and limestone edifice. I attended Cathedral School of Saint Joseph for several years and spent much time in the original edifice. Many years later, I was married in the new Cathedral." Hartford architectural historians Gregory F. Andrews and David F. Ransom believed that "while at first the [new] building appears stark, closer examination reveals a wealth of symbolic and decorative embellishment." There's a legend about the old building that purports any brownstone used in a stonewall throughout the Hartford region came from the burned cathedral, one of the many designed by Patrick C. Keely. In the new cathedral's nave twenty-six oversize windows turn entering light into a blueish tint. The effect is quite heavenly. Only in Hartford: while construction occurred during the late 50s on the new cathedral, congregants met for weekly mass in the auditorium of the Aetna Life Insurance Company. The site adjacent to the new cathedral, the former home of the Cathedral School, now houses Malta House of Care, a clinic where the uninsured can seek health assistance and solace.

Phoenix Mutual Building

American Row

If viewed from just the right position, the lenticular hyperboloid that is the Phoenix Mutual Building does indeed resemble a ship moving forward full speed ahead. The building site matches that of the meeting house of 1636. As Connecticut author Herbert J. Stoeckel wrote, the "building stands almost as an abstract monument to the first boat that came up the Connecticut River." Designed by Harrison & Abramovitz, the "boat building," the world's first two-sided office tower, constructed of glass and steel and thirteen stories, anchored the redevelopment known as Constitution Plaza. The Phoenix's decision to remain in downtown Hartford (its former 1920 building had a very square palazzo design) at a time when the suburbs drew other companies, guaranteed the mid-sixties revitalization efforts. However, these plans catered to car culture, providing in the case of the Phoenix 300 enclosed parking spaces. As the *Courant* noted in 1963, "the typical driver will pass only one light and a half-block of downtown before entering the parking area." At the time, those were words of great praise whereas today we think of that automobile orientation as a key failure. Designed for efficient corporate operations, the structure's distinctive shape attempted to maximize workflow. When first opened, the company used only certain floors and rented others, offering the opportunity for later growth. During its first year, 12,000 visitors toured the building which, like Travelers, allowed visitors to enjoy an observation area with spectacular views. Renovated in 2010, Nassau Reinsurance Group acquired it in 2016. Today the "boat building" remains a beautiful architectural example of late Modernist style and reflections in its blue-green glass form ever-moving cityscapes.

Unitarian Meeting House

Bloomfield Avenue

If Victor Lundy's modernist forms are architecture as sculpture, then one should be able to stroll leisurely around their circumference always appreciating different perspectives. If Lundy's churches of 1956-1962 embody a theologically inspired aspirational architecture, then congregants should be uplifted by the building. The Hartford meeting house's northwest location adjacent to other institutions is not bucolic enough to meet its sculptural intentions. One long-time member told us that members' feelings regarding the design "are of two sorts. The symbolism," he said, "is much appreciated with the buttresses illustrating paths to the truth, the emphasis on the materials and the open peripheral rooms indicating a religion focused on our current world more than the hereafter. But" he continued, "certain design flaws in the roof cavity over the sanctuary failed and were a source of leaking notwithstanding continuing efforts for correction over the years." Suspended by cables from John A. Roebling's Sons Company of New York, the faulty roof sways and creaks. At the same time that Lundy designed this meeting house and four years earlier a similar one in Westport, Connecticut, he also used similar techniques of concrete, metal, and wood for an I. Miller Showroom on Fifth Avenue and the Singer Company Showroom at Rockefeller Center. Does this stylistic juxtaposition of commercial and religious building diminish the spiritual intent of Lundy's meeting house design?

Bushnell Tower

Gold Street

Hartford has too many roads—big and small—for such a small place (18 square miles). Organizations such as Riverfront Recapture, iQuilt, and Hartford 400 acknowledge this and attempt to rectify the problem. The 1969 I. M. Pei 27-story tower of reinforced concrete stands isolated from its surroundings. The building rises from a flat concrete surface with a moat encirclement of tar. The design elements of large windows and balconies resemble Pei's Society Hill Towers of Philadelphia. The latter are more successful, for they form a unit of three with low rise townhouses of corresponding design that transition into, and compliment, the historic neighborhood. In Hartford, a mostly unused and inaccessible concrete elevated terrace further isolates the tower from the city in which it has a visual presence, but not a vibrant one. It is a mirage seen from the curving paths of Bushnell Park. And yet these residences can become a cornerstone to Hartford's residential revival as empty offices, along with in-fill development, offer new places to live and promise urban rejuvenation.

Jacobs Life Sciences Center

Trinity College

Intentionally designed to echo Trinity's late-nineteenth-century example of collegiate Gothic architecture, the Long Walk, the Orr, DeCossey, Winder Life Science Center of 1969 may more closely resemble Paul Rudolph's famous Yale University Art and Architecture Building of 1961. Trinity's example of Brutalism had been threatened with demolition in 2009, but instead renovations in 2011 included a neuroscience lab. Originally designed for the departments of Biology and Psychology and named in honor of the college's fourteenth president, Albert C. Jacobs, the building received an award from the Connecticut Society of Architects. The jury that year found that "the monumental organization of building form and structure serves very successfully to modulate large external spaces created with neighboring buildings." Though the building appeared in a television soap opera, it might have been put to better use in an episode of *Dr. Who*. The jury also thought that "the coarse texture of the concrete, cast in striated forms and sand blasted, is wholly compatible with the monumental scale of the project." We worried during our visit that if one rubs up against the cast-concrete façade, it'll cut one's skin apart. The building has classrooms, an auditorium, a green house, teaching labs, and research labs. The first-floor window-less classrooms have ceilings so high that they seem like sepulchers or choir-lofts.

Gold Building (One Financial Plaza)

Main Street

David Chase, founder and president of Chase Enterprises, sought to change the skyline and character of Hartford's central business district during the 1970s and 1980s when he developed One Financial Plaza, also known as the Gold Building, as well as the Stilts Building (One Corporate Center), and 280 Trumbull Street. Chase survived concentration camps, escaping into the woods and eventually landing in America and settling in Hartford where he attended Weaver High School. At the time of his death in 2018 at the age of 88, his daughter Cheryl A. Chase said that the Gold Building was especially a source of pride for her father. She said, "He was trying to make Hartford like a larger city, give it a big city feel." This 621,000 square foot 26-story office tower designed by Newhaus & Taylor of Houston, Texas, shines due to its gold-framed, tinted glass-paneled exterior. Inside for many years, United Technologies had its corporate headquarters here. In 1982, UTC bought the building. In 2015, UTC moved its offices to Farmington. The Gold Building has had several owners over the years. In May 2019, LAZ Parking and Shelbourne Global paid $70.5 million for it. Currently, the building has a vacancy rate of less than six percent. That's an improvement from 2015 when it had a thirty percent vacancy. David Chase mentored Alan Lazowski, chairman and chief executive of LAZ, and thus it is no coincidence that Lazowski now co-owns the building and its 1,141-space attached parking garage.

XL Center

Trumbull Street

Storytellers often use the figurative expression "and then the roof caved in" to indicate a negative turn in a story. On January 18, 1978, the roof of the Hartford Civic Center, as the XL Center was then known, collapsed. An innovative "space truss" scheme meant to save the city some money failed under the weight of a massive snowstorm. Two years later, with a new roof design and expanded capacity, the Civic Center re-opened. The complex included a below-ground exhibition space, a retail mall featuring Luettgens, a two-story specialty fashion department store, and an attached twenty-two-story hotel. Professional and college sports teams competed in the fifteen-thousand seat arena and top-tier entertainers performed. With three stories below ground and three stories above, the Kling & Associates original plan attempted to fit the urban landscape, but on two-sides the massive windowless structure creates a dark claustrophobic corridor, especially along Church Street. With the addition of Hartford 21, the complex meant to be low-rise now at thirty-six floors has become the fourth highest in the city. The arena itself requires constant upkeep and additional funds. As Michael Freimuth, executive director of the Capital Region Development Authority, said in March 2022, "the minute we get done with [current repairs] something will break." Aetna Life & Casualty envisioned this four-block development as a key to downtown revitalization. It has been and continues to be a great success for drawing suburbanites into town, but most likely provides little enrichment for the residents of the city.

Hartford Stage

Church Street

The architectural historian Charles Jencks once described postmodernism as modernism plus something else. The Hartford Stage as originally designed and built exemplified this description. It used to be a Robert Venturi decorated shed: a modernist box with symbolism. At its entrance on Church Street, it had an oversize Doric column and large bright red signage. When Jeter Cook & Jepson renovated the 1977 building in 2013, they kept the signage but did away with the column, something like removing the steeple from Center Church. The firm noted that "Intervention to the exterior balanced respect for Venturi's design with creating a new and more dynamic connection to the city and providing a better patron experience." One may quibble about the removal of the column, but inside new seating, improved sightlines, and additional gathering space have succeeded in making the bare-bones interior more welcoming to audiences. And with that large signage still blazing away outside, the Hartford Stage remains, to borrow a phrase from the manifesto of the original architects, "an architecture which abandons pure form in favor of mixed media."

Hartford Seminary

Sherman Street

The architectural gem that is the main building at the Hartford Seminary, now known as Hartford International University for Religion and Peace, equals in presence the Connecticut State Capitol and the Travelers Tower. Located on a quiet Westend street, this masterpiece designed by Richard Meier expresses a modernist post-Bauhaus industrial aesthetic that is nonetheless warm and inviting due to its complex play of light and geometry. In 1981 when the building opened the nearly 150-year-old institution transitioned from a training school for Congregational ministers to an emphasis on cross-faith international understanding. The visually stark but striking porcelain-enamel construction combined with a patterned fenestration reminds us of Piet Mondrian's Wadsworth Atheneum *Composition in Blue and White* (1935). Meier even placed a small blue rectangle, Mondrian-like, in the building's chapel. We particularly enjoy the multitude of different planes of sight that characterize this structure's conjoining of inside and outside. In the Hartford Seminary building, Richard Meier has successfully created a place that encourages learning and reflection in spiritual surroundings.

Hartford Steam Boiler

State Street

Viewed from the east along the Connecticut River, this 1983 building, designed by Owens, Skidmore & Merrill, has a fluid, curved shape. Yet from the opposite side the building appears as a series of serrated setbacks. Along with the nearby Pelli-designed Science Center, the view has pleasant and impressive qualities. Much of the appeal comes from the combination of honed and polished Napoleon red granite on the Steam Boiler building. The 500,000 square foot, 24-story office tower has always had other tenants in addition to the one whose logo graces its top. HSB purchased its own headquarters in 2014, but by that time Munich RE had purchased HSB (2009). In 2001, the company donated its large collection of Connecticut Impressionists paintings to the Florence Griswold Museum. The corporation leader at the time, Wilson Wilde, said, "Out of nearly 4,000 employees, more than 2,500 are scientists, engineers, and technicians. We operate from the strong conviction that both the insurance company and the client are happier if nothing happens. That's why we're devoted to *preventing* loss in the first place." The State Street building came after fifty years' use of Carl J. Malmfeldt's Art Deco building on Prospect Street. Fifty years of use: might then the company soon consider another move?

Connecticut Children's Medical Center

Washington Street

"Nowhere have I seen so many parking lots," Jean-Paul Sartre observed during his mid-1940s travels in America. He believed parking lots emblematic of the disjointed and fragmented American city. In Hartford, Connecticut Children's Medical Center expands from its eye-catching original building and the expansion necessitates more parking. There are other challenges in hospital construction. Is it possible to construct buildings that foster clinical efficiency and are also patient friendly, especially where children and their families are the intended beneficiaries of the institution's mission? When planning the hospital, architects wisely studied children's museums, toy stores, and theme parks. "The result," according to a *Hartford Courant* article from February 1996, "is a colorful modern-day castle punctuated with cubes, spheres and cones" – a welcoming building during stressful times of illness. HKS of Dallas received awards from the American Institute of Architects and other organizations for the design. Waiting rooms continue the use of a bright palette and have child size furniture. There are kid friendly activities to occupy (and distract) the patient's siblings. Patient rooms have large windows for light and pullout sofa-beds for parents to stay overnight with their child. This first free-standing comprehensive hospital for children in Connecticut came to completion ahead of schedule and under budget. Additions and improvements followed such as the 2015 Family Resource Center, another facility designed with children in mind and in bright colors. The initial 124-bed eight-story hospital combined personnel, specialized programs, and technologies from Hartford Hospital, UCONN Health Center, and the former Newington Children's Hospital. Children transported by helicopter are first stabilized at the adjoining Hartford Hospital where there is a landing pad and then they are whisked through an underground tunnel to the Children's Hospital where they receive comprehensive sophisticated care in an environment created specifically for them.

Front Street District

Near the start of this century, Hartford crooner Tony Allen told the *Hartford Courant*, "Whatever you wanted was there on Front Street … tailor shops, Italian markets, pawnshops …. " Allen evoked the old neighborhood in his signature song, "I Remember Front Street." Remember is all a person can do. As Gian Lombardo says in his poem, "Who hangs out a window, calling others home, / when the panes are shattered and frames splin- / tered?" Adriaen's Landing redevelopment has failed. Like other revitalization plans, this demolition enhanced the wealth of a few, not the citizens of the city, citizens who had little say in these plans. The Capital City Economic Development Authority (now known as the Capital Region Development Authority) directed these efforts, not the city of Hartford. Expenditures did not make housing more affordable for Hartford's working class nor encouraged their children's education. Front Street / Adriaen's Landing erased history and renders present reality invisible to affluent visitors. The commercial venues currently on-site—a few restaurants, a concert hall, and a now out-of-business movie theater—draw sparse crowds except on occasion when a suburban audience attends an event in the area. Otherwise on a typical day one wonders how they stay in business. The contemporary architecture of some buildings resembles late shopping-mall aesthetic with faux stone facades concrete-formed and a few dark arcades to nowhere. The yesteryear of Front Street—a lively neighborhood of shops and homes and most of all, of people—prospers no more.

Dunkin' Park

Main Street

On April 13, 2017, the Hartford Yard Goats lost 7-2 against the New Hampshire Fisher Cats in their first game at Dunkin' Donuts Park (as it was then known). The home opener at the ballpark had been a year late and the construction at least $11 million over-budget. But was it a complete loss? Hardly. The stadium received the 2017 best Double-A ballpark of the Year award and again several more times after that. Yet, the more than six thousand-seat stadium, which in 2023 sold out forty-four times, has not sparked the anticipated full-scale redevelopment of the surrounding north Hartford area due to an unforeseen and long-lasting lawsuit filed by the stadium's original developer Centerplan Company (though the 270-unit Pennant apartments may point to the sort of development that will be possible here and the late October 2023 final settlement that cost the city $10 million should put an end to legal struggles and allow full-scale development to commence). Despite the legal morass, the stadium's design has been a homerun with the public. The park's distinctive Dunkin' sign overlooks the major intersection of Main and Trumbull. At the entrance the team store as well as concession stands are on the left and a view of the field from the right completes an open concourse concept. Thoughtful placement of seating provides good access to all on-field action no matter where one sits. Even the signage at the stadium is an integral part of the overall architectural plan. Concessions include local vendors such as Scott's Jamaican Bakery and Bear's Smokehouse BBQ. Many game-day employees come from the immediate area, including the Clay Arsenal neighborhood. Even though the parcel posed a challenge with only six sloping acres, the final product with careful positioning and use of bricks, concrete panels, and windows on the exterior keep it in concert with the neighborhood. The ballpark's modest height also blends well with the existing (and potential) surroundings. Josh Solomon, the team owner, said, "We needed for this park to be an impetus for real growth in this part of the city, and it will do that."

Hartford HealthCare Bone & Joint Institute

Seymour Street

The British architects Paul James and Tony Noakes have written, "The functional and technical complexity of modern hospitals has often led to the neglect of aesthetic quality." Yet, they believe "there is scope for architects to bring pleasure to experiences which are inherently anxious or painful for patients, and to the working life of dedicated staff carrying out difficult and stressful tasks." The design language of the Bone & Joint Institute intended to evoke a patient-centered experience. But still the battleship gray exterior panels and the structural allusion to a human joint do little to welcome incoming patients. Similarly, the interior space of this 130,000 square foot facility lacks character despite some wood-clad features and examination rooms are small square institutional boxes devoid of warmth. Nevertheless, the building received several awards upon its completion and the Institute represents a good effort by Harford HealthCare to be a good civic-minded corporate citizen. Today hospital buildings loom threateningly over urban neighborhoods. Hartford HealthCare owns many abandoned historic properties in its Frog Hollow neighborhood. Marcus Ordoñez, co-chair of the Frog Hollow Neighborhood Revitalization Zone, told the *Hartford Courant* that hospital structures should "not only benefit the patients … but the neighborhood." While a well-designed building may contribute to patients' well-being and employee performance, too often results are a mishmash of buildings in mediocre campus settings and paved over neighborhoods for surface lots or garage parking.

UCONN Hartford

Prospect Street

Here at the end of this tribute to Hartford, we return to Donn Barber, a City Beautiful architect whose buildings enrich our urban landscape. In particular, the Hartford Times Building (1920) with its colorful Beaux-Arts classicism now anchors the successful downtown UCONN campus. Ironically, the Times Building incorporated elements from a demolished New York McKim, Meade & White church. This is ironic because after the newspaper ceased publication in 1976, on occasion the building was threatened with demolition. For a time, the city of Hartford used it and at the start of this century, after the collapse of the Caroline Bos and Ben Van Berkel plan to reimagine the Wadsworth Atheneum, the museum considered incorporating the Times Building into its campus. In 2014, UCONN approved relocation of its West Hartford campus to a renovated and enlarged Times Building. The architectural firm headed by Robert A. M. Stern, former dean of the Yale School of Architecture, designed the award-winning project. In addition to modern day features needed by a college campus, the task also included stabilizing the façade and murals on the portico walls and other repairs. University architect Laura Cruickshank said, "Everyone worked together, and the result is a restored iconic building that houses a vibrant academic program." The 179,000 square foot complex with a stunning atrium at its center, has achieved LEED Gold certification. On the exterior, buff-colored masonry and metal and glass compliment Barber's original construction. Always a beacon of education and information, the Hartford Times Building, now UCONN Hartford, provides the impetus for the city's better future by way of the students who learn and then take that knowledge out into the city and beyond.

Notes on Contributors

DENNIS BARONE's recent works include *A Field Guide to the Rehearsal* (2022) and *After Math* (2023). He is the current Poetry Editor of the *Wallace Stevens Journal* and Professor Emeritus in English at the University of Saint Joseph.

CHRISTINE BECK worked as a lawyer for twenty-years and then turned to teaching and poetry. She started the Poets on Poetry program of the Connecticut Poetry Society and is the author of *Stirred, Not Shaken* and other works.

CIARAN BERRY is a Professor of English at Trinity College where he directs the program in creative writing. His most recent book is *Liner Notes*.

ANTOINETTE BRIM-BELL, Connecticut's eighth State Poet Laureate, is the author of three books of poetry as well as a printmaker and collage artist. Brim-Bell is a Professor of English at Capital Community College.

DAVID CAPPELLA is a Professor Emeritus in English at Central Connecticut State University. He is co-author of two books on the teaching of poetry. His sonnet sequence loosely based on the life of Giacomo Leopardi, *Gobbo: A Solitaire's Opera*, was published during 2022 in both an English and an English / Italian version.

SHARON L. CHARDE's *The Glass is Already Broken* was published in 2021. She is a retired psychotherapist and writing teacher.

BRIAN CLEMENTS is a Professor and Director of the Kathwari Honors Program at Western Connecticut State University. His most recent collection of poems is *A Book of Common Rituals*, and he is co-editor of *Bullets into Bells: Poets & Citizens Respond to Gun Violence*.

TOM CONDON writes about urban and regional issues for the CT Mirror. He worked as a reporter, columnist, and editor at the *Hartford Courant* for forty-five years. He was elected to the New England Newspaper Hall of Fame in 2016.

GINNY LOWE CONNORS is the publisher of Grayson Books as well as a former Poet Laureate of West Hartford. She has authored several books of poetry and edited a number of poetry anthologies. Her most recent poetry collection is *Without Goodbyes: From Puritan Deerfield to Mohawk Kahnawake.*

BRAD DAVIS, an Episcopal minister, was chaplain, squash coach, and teacher at the Pomfret School for many years. His most recent collection is *On the Way to Putnam: New, Selected, & Early Poems.*

RICHARD DEMING is a poet, art critic, and theorist whose work explores the intersections of poetry, philosophy, and visual culture. He is the director of Creative Writing at Yale University and author of *Day for Night* among other works.

KENNETH DIMAGGIO is a retired Professor of Humanities at Capital Community College. His poems have appeared in *The Chiron Review*, *The Paterson Literary Review*, and elsewhere. He grew up in the capital region, attended Colorado State University and the University of Iowa, and then returned to Hartford.

DANIEL DONAGHY is a Professor of English at Eastern Connecticut State University and a prize-winning poet. He is the author of five poetry collections, most recently *Somerset.*

DEBORAH DUCOFF-BARONE, a former curator at the Museum of Connecticut History, has worked for corporations such as The Hartford and Pratt and Whitney. She holds a PhD in American Civilization from the University of Pennsylvania and currently serves as president of the League of Women Voters of Greater Hartford.

ANITA DURKIN, Visitor Experience and Education Senior Coordinator at the Harriet Beecher Stowe Center, has a PhD in American Literature from the University of Rochester, and has published poems in *Atlas & Alice* and *The Wallace Stevens Journal* and critical essays in the *African American Review* and *Arizona Quarterly*.

DAVID EPSTEIN has a PhD in literature from Brandeis University. He has published poems in *The Lyric, Marsh Hawk Review, Shofar*, and elsewhere.

JAMES FINNEGAN is a former Poet Laureate of West Hartford. He is well-known in the Hartford region for hosting several reading series, currently the Word House series at the Noah Webster House. His poems have appeared in *Ploughshares, The Southern Review*, and other journals. He is the co-editor (with Dennis Barone) of *Visiting Wallace: Poems Inspired by the Life and Work of Wallace Stevens*.

DONNA FLEISCHER's poetry books include *Periodic Earth* (2016) and *Twinkle, Twinkle* (2011). Her poems earned a Massachusetts Museum of Contemporary Art (MassMoCA)—Tupelo Press residency and first prize awards for haiku from the Board of Education, City of Nagoya, Japan and the University of Hartford Writing Award for Poetry.

SEAN FREDERICK FORBES is director of the Creative Writing Program at the University of Connecticut, Storrs. He is the author of *Providencia* and co-editor of *The Beiging of America: Personal Narratives About Being Mixed Race in the 21st Century*.

CHARLES FORT is the author of *We Did Not Fear the Father: New and Selects Poems* and other books. He grew up in New Britain, taught for many years at the University of Nebraska at Kearney, and received an Honorary Doctorate of Humane Letters, *honoris causa*, from Siena Heights University.

MARGARET GIBSON is a former Connecticut State Poet Laureate and Professor Emerita, University of Connecticut. Among her many publications are the trilogy *Broken Cup*, *Not Hearing the Wood Thrush*, and *The Glass Globe*.

BENJAMIN S. GROSSBERG is a Professor of English at the University of Hartford where he directs the program in Creative Writing. His recent book *My Husband Would* received a Connecticut Book Award.

ASIA HAMILTON received the 2023 Wallace Stevens Scholarship Award presented by the Hartford Friends of Wallace Stevens. She is a graduate of Weaver High School and currently attends Trinity College.

JOAN HOFMANN, Professor Emerita at the University of Saint Joseph, was the first Poet Laureate of Canton, Connecticut. She is the author of three chapbooks, most recently, *Alive, Too*.

SUSAN HOWE received the prestigious Bollingen Prize in American Poetry in 2011. Among her many publications are *My Emily Dickinson*, *The Midnight*, and *The Quarry*.

CATHERINE E. HOYSER is a Professor Emerita of English at the University of Saint Joseph where she directed the Women's Studies Program. She has written on feminist pedagogy as well as Lady Gaga and Tom Robbins. Her poems have been published in *The Paterson Literary Review* and elsewhere.

BRIAN JOHNSON is a Professor of English at Southern Connecticut State University where he has served as President of the Faculty Senate. Among his published works is *Site Visits*, a collaboration with a German painter.

MARILYN E. JOHNSTON, born and raised in Hartford, worked in corporate communications and then for the Bloomfield Library. She is the author of *Weight of the Angel* and other works.

FREDERICK-DOUGLAS KNOWLES II is a Professor of English at Three Rivers Community College and the inaugural Poet Laureate of Hartford. He is the author of *BlackRoseCity*.

GIAN LOMBARDO, Senior Publisher-in-Residence at Emerson College, directs Quale Press. He is an advocate for prose poetry and has published many books as author, editor, or translator, including *Gaspard de la Nuit* by Louis Bertrand.

JOHN LONG lived in Hartford in the late 1970s. He is a poet and playwright. His work has appeared in the *Connecticut River Review*, *Dark Horse*, and the *Hartford Courant*. John's plays have been produced at the Ensemble Studio Theater, the Phoenix Stage Company, and elsewhere. He lectured in Drama and Film at the Torrington and Waterbury campuses of the University of Connecticut.

SRINIVAS MANDAVILLI is the Chief of Pathology and Laboratory Medicine at Hartford Hospital. He has published his poems in many journals and is the author of *Gods in the Foyer*.

TOM NICOTERA has published poems in numerous small press publications, and his poems have been performed by the East Haddam Stage Co. He was a co-founder of Bloomfield Library's Wintonbury Poetry Series. His poetry book *What Better Place To Be Than Here?* was published by Foothills Publishing in 2015.

JULIA M. PAUL has served as the first Poet Laureate of Manchester, Connecticut. She is the author of the poetry books *Shook*, *Staring Down the Tracks*, and *Table with Burning Candle*. A strong believer in poetry as a powerful and necessary form of communication, Paul leads the Riverwood Poetry Series, a long-running poetry reading series in Hartford, Connecticut.

BESSY REYNA, a poet, memoirist, and cultural critic, has published her writing both in the US and Mexico. Born in Cuba and raised in Panama, she is a graduate of Mt. Holyoke College and the University of Connecticut School of Law. She was inducted into the Immigrant Heritage Hall of Fame in 2017.

CLARE ROSSINI recently retired as Artist-in-Residence in the English Department at Trinity College. She has published three volumes of poetry, the most recent of which is *Lingo*. With Benjamin S. Grossberg she co-edited *The Poetry of Capital: Voices from Twenty-First Century America*.

MARIA SASSI served as the first poet laureate of West Hartford. She is the author of *Rooted in Stars* and *Rare Grasses*. She has hosted poetry readings at the Noah Webster House, the Old State House, and the Charter Oak Cultural Center.

PEGI DEITZ SHEA, known for exploring human rights issues in children's books, says that "I was first and foremost a writer of poetry for adult readers." She was the first Poet Laureate of Vernon, CT and is the author of the poetry collection *The Weight of Kindling*.

JOHN L. STANIZZI teaches literature at Manchester Community College. Among his many books are *Pond*, *Hallelujah Time*, and *See*.

STEVE STRAIGHT's collection *Affirmation* received the 2023 William Meredith Award in Poetry. He is a retired professor of English and former director of the poetry program at Manchester Community College.

JULIEN STRONG is an Assistant Professor of English at Central Connecticut State University and the author of four books, including the poetry collections *Tour of the Breath Gallery* and *The Mouth of Earth*.

JOHN SUROWIECKI has worked as a journalist, copywriter, and teacher. He has published fiction and poetry including *The Place of Solitaires: Poems from Titles by Wallace Stevens*.

ELIZABETH THOMAS is a poet, educator, and arts advocate. She is the founder of UpWords Poetry, a company dedicated to promoting programs for young writers and educators, and author of several books of poetry including *From the Front of the Classroom*.

CHASE TWICHELL was born in New Haven, earned her BA from Trintiy College and MFA from the Iowa Writers' Workshop. In 1999 she founded Ausable Press. Among her own books are *Things as It Is* and *Horses Where the Answers Should Have Been* which received the Kingsley Tufts Poetry Award.

Poet and artist SALLY VAN DOREN was awarded the 2007 Walt Whitman Award from the Academy of American Poets for her first collection of poems, *Sex at Noon Taxes*. She serves on the board of the Five Points Center for the Visual Arts in Torrington, Connecticut.

DAVYNE VERSTANDIG directed UConn's Litchfield County Writers Project for many years. She was the Poet Laureate of Washington, Connecticut and is the author of *Pieces of the Whole* and *Provisions*.

Permissions

Dennis Barone: "Perfect Six" copyright © 2011 by Dennis Barone, from *Parallel Lines*, published by Shearsman Books, Ltd. in 2011. Used by permission of the author.

Dennis Barone and Deborah Ducoff-Barone. Descriptions of Buildings. Copyright © 2024 by the authors. Used by permission of the authors.

Christine Beck: "Hartford Public Library" copyright © 2024 by the author. Used by permission of the author.

Ciaran Berry: "Prince Rogers Nelson Live at the Albert C. Jacobs Life Sciences Center" copyright © 2024 by the author. Used by permission of the author.

Antoinette Brim-Bell: "Song for the Talcott Street Congregational Church" copyright © 2024 by the author. Used by permission of the author.

David Cappella: "The Hartford Steam Boiler Building" copyright © 2024 by the author. Used by permission of the author.

Sharon L. Charde: "There Used to Be Music" copyright © 2024 by the author. Used by permission of the author.

Brian Clements: "Poems about buildings" copyright © 2024 by the author. Used by permission of the author.

Tom Condon. "Preface" Copyright © 2024 by the author. Used by permission of the author.

Ginny Lowe Connors: "The Mark Twain House" copyright © 2024 by the author. Used by permission of the author.

Brad Davis: "Over on Woodland" copyright © 2024 by the author. Used by permission of the author.

Richard Deming: "Of Stevens and The Hartford in Morning Light" copyright © 2024 by the author. Used by permission of the author.

Kenneth DiMaggio: "Ode to the G. Fox Department Store in Hartford" copyright © 2024 by the author. Used by permission of the author.